AN ILLUSTRATED HISTORY OF THAMES PLEASURE STEAMERS

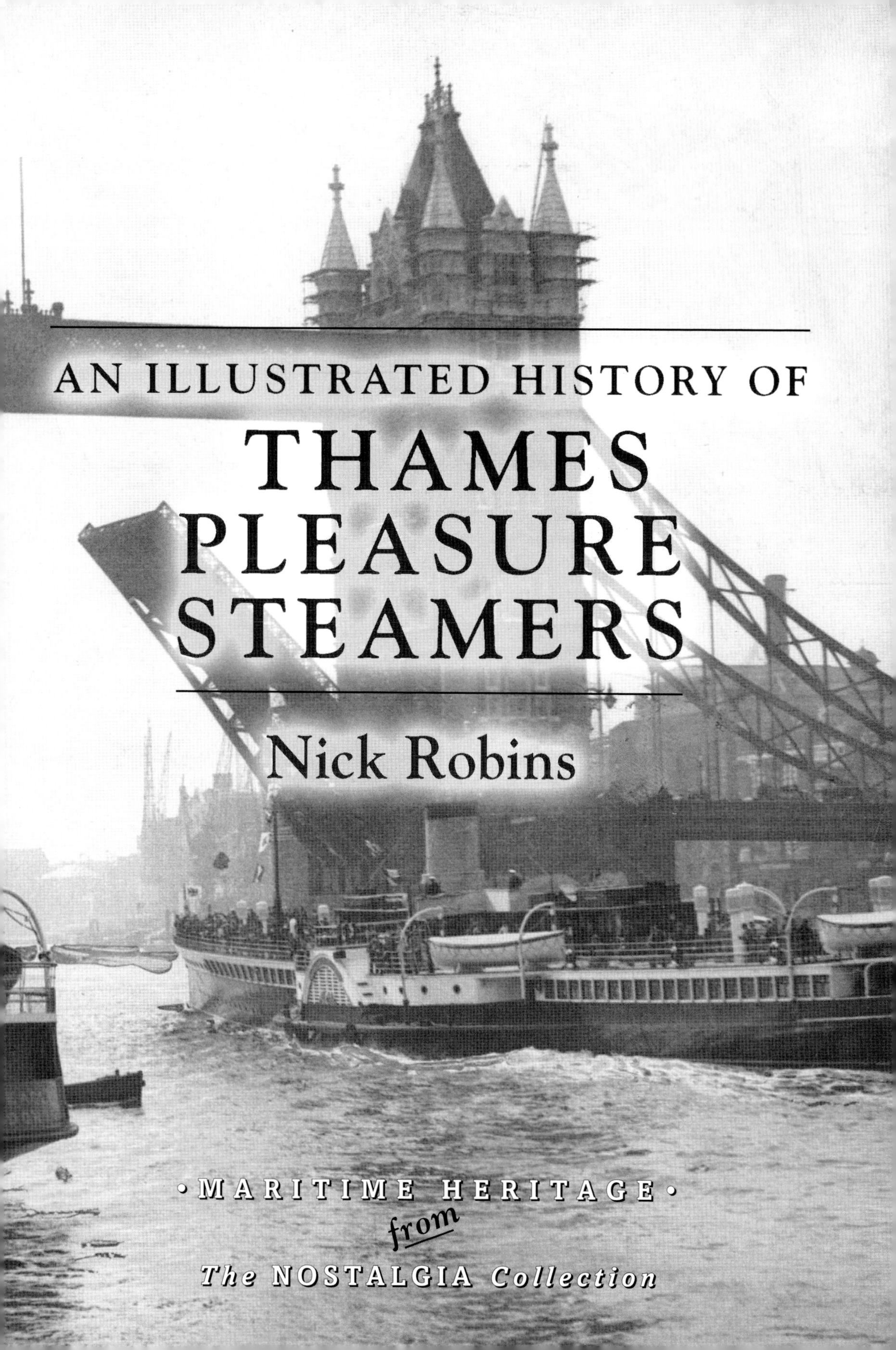

AN ILLUSTRATED HISTORY OF

THAMES PLEASURE STEAMERS

Nick Robins

• MARITIME HERITAGE •
from
The NOSTALGIA Collection

First published in 2009

British Library Cataloguing in Publication Data

A catalogue record for this book is available from the British Library.

ISBN 978 1 85794 318 4

Silver Link Publishing Ltd
The Trundle
Ringstead Road
Great Addington
Kettering
Northants NN14 4BW

Tel/Fax: 01536 330588
email: sales@nostalgiacollection.com
Website: www.nostalgiacollection.com

Printed and bound in the Czech Republic

Unless otherwise credited all photographs are from the author's collection.

Title page **Royal Eagle (1932) and *Crested Eagle* (1925) in the Pool of London.** *DP World P&O Heritage Collection*

Below **The former Thames paddle steamer *La Marguerite* (1894) leaves Garth Pier at Bangor while registered at Liverpool under the ownership of the Liverpool & North Wales Steamship Company.** *Bob Drewett collection*

Below right **The *Royal Sovereign* (1893) and *Koh-I-Noor* (1892) at their moorings off Charing Cross.**

CONTENTS

The *Royal Eagle* (1932) backing away from Tower Pier with crowded decks. *DP World P&O Heritage Collection*

PREFACE

My boyhood summer holidays were normally spent at Leigh-on-Sea, preceded by an exciting rail journey from Manchester to St Pancras and across to Fenchurch Street. From London to Leigh the train would sing 'Grandma's seaside, Grandma's seaside' as we caught our first glimpse of the sea. But the highlights of the two-week family holiday were the rail and sea trip sailing from Tower Pier to Southend and perhaps a day trip to Margate, both usually taken by the *Royal Sovereign*, and best of all the afternoon cruise to Herne Bay aboard the *Medway Queen*. I suppose Southend Pier was my boyhood Mecca.

Given these memories it has been natural in recent years to read the stories written about the Thames 'butterfly boats'. The history of the Thames excursion ships has been told in different ways by different authors, and the time is right to bring the story up to date and to place all the events and happenings into their appropriate historical context.

It is an ongoing story that starts in 1814 when the first steamer arrived in the Thames to ply her trade. The story continues today with the annual visits of the *Waverley* and the *Balmoral*, as well as the down-river excursion programmes offered by the *Princess Pocahontas* and the river steamer *Kingswear Castle*. It is an exciting story that encompasses triumph and disaster as well as intrigue and financial trickery. This history is dedicated to the men and women who served in the Thames steamers to bring so much pleasure to millions of excursionists, but who also conducted themselves with great honour during two World Wars.

Although the author is given the credit for having produced a book of this kind, it should be remembered that it is very much a team effort. The publisher and the book designer are key to the success of any book, and the author is reliant on a team of friends and associates who assist him in gathering information and photographic material. The author particularly thanks Richard Danielson, and Iain Hope for assistance in unravelling some of the mysteries, as well as George Gardner at Glasgow University Archive Services and Stephen Rabson, P&O Historian and Archivist, DP World. The assistance provided by Iain Hope of Blewbury and Professor Donald Meek in Falkirk, by reading, checking, correcting and adding to the manuscript, has been invaluable – thank you both.

Nick Robins
Crowmarsh
Oxfordshire

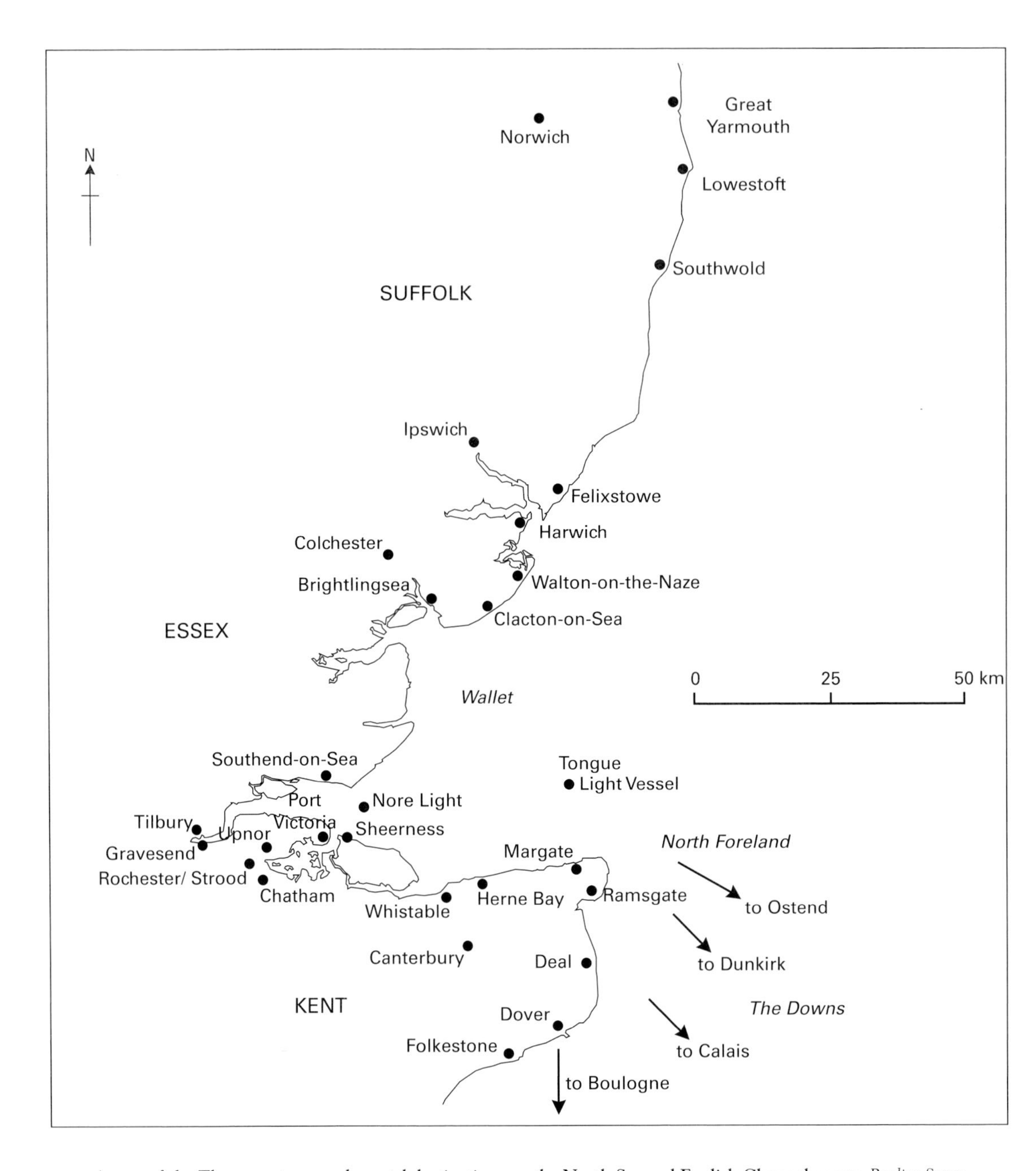

A map of the Thames estuary and coastal destinations on the North Sea and English Channel coasts. *Pauline Sapey*

1. THE STEAM PACKET COMES TO THE THAMES

'...but in 1814, a Mr Lawrence did run a steamboat between Bristol and Bath, which was transferred by inland navigation to the Thames. The opposition met with from the Thames watermen obliged the little vessel to return to Bristol. The early steamboats were not at first a success. Interruptions continually took place. The old watermen did everything they could to obstruct. Machinery frequently broke down. The working expenses were heavy. But the end was inevitable and in 1834 the last of the tilt [rowing] boats, the *Duke of York*, was withdrawn.'

Frank Burtt, *Steamers of the Thames and Medway*, 1949

Until the arrival of the steam packet, communication between London and the major centres along the south Thames coast was by sailing packet, known locally as a 'Margate Hoy', and as far as Gravesend by a 'tilt' boat, a rowing boat with an awning or tilt. Dependent on favourable winds and tides, the hoy could take up to a week to get down river to Margate, having called at Gravesend and Sheerness en route. A little wooden steamer, however, could guarantee arrival at Margate the same day and a return trip to Hammersmith by evening the next day. Travel to centres in Essex, however, remained dependent on the stagecoach, with access to the river hindered by Dickens's famous Essex Marshes, although small boats could get to both Chelmsford and Colchester.

One of the first steamers to be seen at London was the *Richmond*, owned by George Dodd. She was a small river paddler, and was placed on a service between Richmond and Hammersmith in 1814, just two years after the successful trials of Henry Bell's *Comet* on the Clyde, and one year before the end of the Napoleonic Wars. The little *Richmond* had a 10 horsepower engine, and the 'great frost' of 1814/15 did little to help her battles against the tides when the river froze over at Blackfriars. When a steam pipe burst, the watermen made loud claims that the steam engine was a danger to all, and that the *Richmond* should not be allowed on the river.

The coming of the steamer had not been all good news as the watermen and boatmen of the Thames, recognising immediately that their very existence could be under threat, did everything they could to hinder the progress and acceptance of the new technology. The travelling public, however, thought otherwise and the steamer was allowed to stay.

The first sea-going packet was the wooden paddle steamer *Marjory*, which arrived from her builders on the Clyde in January 1815, having travelled through the North Sea via the Forth & Clyde Canal. Her arrival marked the entry of the steamship into service on the lower Thames and a long association between Clyde shipbuilders and ship-owners with the steam packets and subsequent excursion ships that have since served the Thames piers 'weather and other circumstances permitting'. The *Marjory* was placed on service from Wapping Old Stairs to Milton, where passengers landed by rowing boat. The return trip lasted more than two days and cost a substantial 8 shillings in the chief cabin, but only 4 shillings in the fore cabin.

An advertisement for the *Marjory* on her first sailing on 23 January 1815 read:

'The public are respectfully informed that the new London steam engine packet *Marjory*,

The first commercial European passenger steamer: a replica of Henry Bell's *Comet* at Port Glasgow. *Author*

Captain Cortis, will start precisely at ten o'clock, on Monday morning, the twenty third inst. from Wapping Old Stairs, near the London Docks, to Milton, below Gravesend, and will return from thence at the same hour on the succeeding morning to the same stairs, the said packet having superb accommodation. Passengers and their luggage will be conveyed to and fro with more certain speed and safety, than by any other conveyance by land or water, and on reasonable fares. Passengers are requested to be punctual to the time specified.'

In fact, the *Marjory* tended to miss a lot of sailings, laid up either at Milton or at Wapping while her machinery was repaired and adjusted. To add to the difficulties, Captain Cortis was removed from his vessel and replaced by a Freeman of the Waterman's Company following proceedings under the Waterman's Act. Not surprisingly, this pioneer vessel was withdrawn at the end of the summer while other steamers came into service on the river.

The next steamer to be introduced was the *Argyle*, sometimes reported as the *Duke of Argyle*. A delightful account of early steamers' tentative voyages away from the Clyde is given in Ward Lock & Company's *The Wonder Book of Ships* (undated but about 1926):

'These early steamers, small as they were, were sent on voyages which we should never dream of expecting such vessels to accomplish today. In June 1815, the *Elizabeth*, built in 1813, 58 feet long and of only 8 horse power, went all the way from the Clyde to Liverpool. She was the first British steamer to undertake a sea voyage, and was in charge of a young naval lieutenant named Hargrave and his cousin, neither of which had reached the age of nineteen. The *Elizabeth*'s voyage was most adventurous, but the cousins brought their steamer safely through two gales and reached the Mersey none the worse for their experiences.

In the same year, two vessels steamed from the Clyde to London. One of these, the *Argyle* (afterwards called the *Thames*), carried two passengers from Dublin to London. When the little vessel – she was only 65 feet long and of 70 tons register – put in at Portsmouth, an Admiralty court martial that was then sitting adjourned in haste to see the wonderful sight of a vessel propelled by steam. She was afterwards employed in service between London and Margate.'

The two passengers were Isaac Weld, Secretary of the Royal Dublin Society, and his wife, the latter becoming the first lady to take a cross-channel passage in a steamer. Apparently not only was the court martial at Portsmouth adjourned, but the Commander-in-Chief, three Admirals and a bevy of Captains were taken for a cruise in the vessel. She finally arrived at Limehouse on the evening of 12 June having maintained an average speed of 6 knots. Throughout the voyage Captain George Dodd had been assisted by one engineer and one fireman, a brief stop having been made in the lee of the Welsh coast to rest the stoker and to allow the engineer to oil his engine.

The *Argyle* joined the so called 'Long Ferry' to Gravesend, providing a daily service each way for her new owners, R. Cheesewright & Company. As with the *Marjory*, she had a carvel hull, and a large square sail could be set on the tall funnel pipe under favourable conditions. Her engine consisted of a single vertical cylinder of 24 inches diameter and the piston had a stroke of 36 inches. The cabins opened on to an outside gallery, which, with her gun ports, made the *Argyle* an imposing sight (the French were still considered a threat at that time, the Admiralty preferring to arm merchantmen in readiness for renewed war). She was, by all accounts, both well-appointed and well-received. *The Times* reported on her arrival into service in July 1815:

> 'She is rapid, spacious, and indeed a splendid vessel. Her cabins are large and fitted with all that elegance could suggest or that personal comfort could require. She presents a choice library, and back gammon, draught boards, and other amusements are provided.'

Graham Farr, in his book *West Country Steamers*, describes the *Argyle* as the first steamer to make a call in the Bristol Channel area:

> 'This was the *Duke of Argyle*, built at Port Glasgow in 1814 by Alexander Martin, for the Glasgow to Greenock run. Her engine of 14 horse power was built by the well-known early builder James Cook of Tradestown, and is reported to have given her 6 knots, probably only in smooth water. Her length from an early list was 78½ feet overall, breadth over paddle boxes 22¼ feet, tonnage 74 gross. Her paddle boxes were 8.8 feet in diameter, with floats 4 feet by 1½ feet. In April 1815 she was sold to London owners and left Glasgow in the following month, calling at Dublin, Wexford, Milford Haven and Portsmouth. [Captain George] Dodd's *Dissertation on steam packets* (1818) reprints a diary of the voyage showing that much bad weather was encountered, besides paddle trouble and the inevitable accounts of shore folk thinking she was a vessel on fire. She was subsequently renamed *Thames* and plied at various times between London and Margate, London and Gravesend, and perhaps on the Solent. Some time, probably in 1816, she was lengthened to 90 feet overall (76½ feet between posts), giving her an "old measurement" tonnage of 50 net; at the same time being fitted with 11-foot wheels and 3½-foot floats.'

It was not long before other steamers took up service. There were four at the close of 1815, the *Richmond*, *Argyle*, *Defiance* and *Hope*. The *Defiance* was employed between London and Margate and the *Hope* between London, Sheerness and Chatham. The *Argyle*, renamed *Thames*, ran between London, Gravesend and Margate for the Gravesend Steam Packet. The following year she was replaced by a faster and larger vessel, the *Regent*, 112 tons and engines of 24 nominal horsepower, notable as the first steam boat to have been built on the Thames. Her designer was none other than Brunel. However, just over a year after entering the Margate service she was gutted by fire off Whitstable, as Tim Sherwood describes in his book *The Steamboat Revolution: London's first steamships*:

> '3 July 1817: a notice was posted at Lloyds announcing the loss of the *Regent* steamer, which was bound for Margate. She had caught fire off Whitstable. Fortunately her captain was able to beach her and put his forty passengers and ten crew ashore. The funnel had become overheated – part of the casing had blown off in strong winds – and the decking caught fire. She had cost £11,000 to construct.'

The Gravesend service operated by the *Thames* was advertised as follows, but just why 'Gentlemen in large parties of pleasure' are singled out is not recorded:

> 'The *Thames*, Captain Payne, will leave the Tower Stairs for Gravesend every morning at 8 o'clock (Friday excepted) and return every afternoon at 3 o'clock the same day for London. Fares on Sundays 3/- each, other days best cabin 3/, fore cabin 2/-. Ladies accompanied by Gentlemen in large parties of pleasure, passage free, Sundays only excepted.

Refreshments provided: tea, bottled porter, etc.'

As the steamship became accepted as a more or less reliable form of transport, more and more small companies were set up to operate them. As on the Clyde at this time it was not uncommon for the majority share-owner to double as ship's master, while other companies such as the Gravesend Steam Packet owned and operated more than one ship. In the first ten years of steamship operation, 26 steamers had seen service on the Thames (see Table 1), so that in 1824 at least 15 steamers were on service to Gravesend, Sheerness and Chatham, Southend-on-Sea landing stage (until 1830 just a wooden jetty accessible only at high water), Ramsgate and the fishing port of Margate.

Some of the early packets were distinctive, some failed from the outset, while others gave up to 40 years of service on the river. Among the failures was the *London Engineer*. Burtt (1949) describes the ship as follows:

'Her dimensions were 120 feet long, beam 24 feet, with a draft of 5 feet, tonnage 315. The

Table 1: Steam Packets on the Thames until 1824 (after Burtt, 1949)

Name	Built	Builder	Routes
Marjory	1814	William Denny, Dumbarton	London-Margate; London Gravesend
Richmond	1814	Lepingwell, Yarmouth	Richmond-London
Argyle/Thames	1815	J. & C. Wood, Glasgow	London-Margate; London Gravesend
Defiance	1815		London-Margate
Hope	1815	Lawrence, Bristol	London-Sheerness-Chatham
Regent	1816	Courthope, Rotherhithe	London-Margate
Caledonia	1816	J. & C. Wood, Glasgow	London-Margate
Majestic	1816	Court, Ramsgate	London-Margate
Britannia	1817	Titterton, Stockwith	London-Southend
Sons of Commerce	1817	Lafort, Blackfriars	London-Margate
Favourite	1817	Evans, Rochester	London-Margate
London	1817	Searle, Westminster	Richmond-London Southend-Sheerness
Diana	1817	Brent, Rotherhithe	Richmond-London Southend-Sheerness
Victory	1818	Evans, Rotherhithe	London-Margate
London Engineer	1818	Brent, Rotherhithe	London-Margate
Rapid	1820	Greenock	London-Margate
Eclipse	1820	Brent, Rotherhithe	London-Margate
Eagle	1820	Greenock	London-Margate
Venus	1821	Brent, Rotherhithe	London-Margate
Albion	1821	Evans, Rotherhithe	London-Margate
Swiftsure	1821	Wallis, Blackwall	London-Gravesend
Hero	1821	Bankham, Medway	London-Margate
Sir J. Yorke	1822	Joliffe, Chester	Southend-Sheerness
Royal Sovereign	1822	Brockelbank, Deptford	London-Ramsgate
Dart	1823	Evans, Rotherhithe	London-Margate
City of London	1824	Brockelbank, Deptford	London-Margate

machinery was of peculiar design, being of the bell crank pattern, having two vertical cylinders 36 inches in diameter with a 30-inch stroke. The cylinders were placed on either side of the vessel driving a pair of internal paddle wheels. The two paddles made 28 revolutions per minute, and the stream of water to them was kept constant by air forced into the waterway by two large pumps. The boiler pressure was 5lb per square inch and steam was supplied by three single-furnace copper boilers.'

The *London Engineer* was nicely appointed with upholstered settees in the main cabin, although fore cabin occupants had to make do with wooden benches. She was flush-decked, as were all her contemporaries, but she had a highly ornamented hull, looking to all intents and purposes like a screw steamer. There was ornate scrollwork fore and aft, a bowsprit and a figurehead, the latter best described as a woman wringing her hands (perhaps she knew all along that the ship could not be steered or got up to speed!). The ship's funnel was nearly as tall as her two masts. However, she did not go anywhere fast or in a straight line, and her working career on the Margate run was but brief.

One of the fastest of the early packets was the *Favourite*, her name seemingly an early attempt at marketing. In 1818 the *Favourite* accomplished the first 'day trip' to Margate from London. Sailing at 4.45am, she reached Margate at 2pm and started the return trip 45 minutes later. She returned her 158 passengers safely to the city at 10pm.

A newspaper article entitled 'Early steamboat travelling: a voyage to Margate in 1823', published in 1895, included this description of travelling aboard the *Venus*, operated by the Margate Company and later by GSN:

> '…on board the *Venus* steamboat for Margate when boiling and smoking away in the most agreeable style to the great delight of nearly two hundred cockneys of all ages, sizes and sexes. She (if feminine is the gender of a steamer) arrived in 7½ hours at her destination. The accommodation of this vessel is superior to any sailing vessel I ever saw. Splendid cabins, mahogany fittings, horsehair sofas, carpeted floors, tiers of windows like the ports of a frigate, with bars and bar maids, kitchen and cooks, stewards and waiters and all suitable paraphernalia of splendid breakfasting and dinnering…'

The *Royal Sovereign* and *Hero* were very much the market leaders when delivered from the yard of Thomas Brockelbank at Deptford in the early 1820s. These vessels were more than 130 feet long with gross tonnages of 220 and 233 respectively. However, their most distinguishing feature was that they were the first Thames steamers to have engines that could develop as much as 100 nominal horsepower. Such larger and faster vessels were the direct response to demand, with over a million passengers now using the Thames packets each year. As was the custom of the day, they still carried 12-pounder guns concealed behind ornamented ports. Remarkably the steamer was in charge by 1822, when there was just one last passenger hoy sailing to Margate.

Shipbuilder and timber merchant Thomas Brockelbank entered the London-Margate service when he built and commissioned the *Eagle* in 1820. She was comparatively fast and roomy and her success inspired Brockelbank to a greater vision. With his fleet enhanced to four, he approached other owners to join him in establishing a collaborative venture with the aim of trading even beyond Margate and without geographical limits. At a meeting held in the summer of 1824 was born the General Steam Navigation Company (GSN), which in October that year began trading with five steamers on the London to Margate route. These were Thomas Brockelbank's *Royal Sovereign* and *City of London*, and William Joliffe and Edward Banks's steamers *Earl of Liverpool* and *Lord Melville*, together with the *Victory*, which may only have been on charter to GSN. The *Eagle*, of course, remained in Thomas Brockelbank's ownership, although she is widely and erroneously reported as GSN's very first vessel. By 1825 routes had been opened by GSN to Calais, Boulogne and Ostend, while London-based services to Hamburg and Dunkirk soon followed, and a route between Portsmouth and Le Havre commenced. Fleet expansion included the purchase of three second-hand ships, the *Marchioness*, *Waterloo* and *Belfast*, from George

Langtry of Belfast (precursor to the Belfast Steamship Company). At home the Thames trade developed quickly, as also did the competition, and by 1830 there was a total of 17 steamers competing for the Margate trade, of which all but five belonged to GSN.

GSN and Thomas Brockelbank (1774-1843)

Thomas Brockelbank was a self-made man who had built up a timber yard at Deptford, which in due course led him to shipbuilding at a nearby site at Deptford Creek. With his brother John he was instrumental in canvassing for the merger of shipping interests, which, with the collaboration of William John Hall in 1824, became the General Steam Navigation Company (not to be confused with Thomas and Jno. Brocklebank from Ontario, founders of the liner company of the same name).

Eighteen directors were elected to the board of the new company. A prospectus was sent to His Majesty's Ministers, members of both Houses of Parliament, to various bankers, the Directors of the East India Company, to the Lord Mayor and Court of Aldermen of the City of London, to principal maritime organisations and to Lloyds at the Royal Exchange. William Hall was operating vessels between London and Hull, but apart from Hall and, of course, Thomas Brockelbank, none of the other Directors had previously been involved in shipping. The initial share issue gave the company an immediate working capital of £50,000, rising to £2 million should the full value of the 20,000 shares be called in.

The prospectus stated that the new company, to be known as the General Steam Navigation Company, would trade to India, America and countries bordering on the North Sea and the English Channel. It eventually limited its routes to UK coastal, the Continent and the Mediterranean, although occasional voyages were taken to Canada and Africa as trade demanded. By 1837 GSN owned 40 vessels including the Thames packets, and in 1837 the company had commissioned one of the very first iron-hulled sea-going steamers, the *Rainbow*. Alan Peake, writing in *Lloyds' Log* in 1974, describes Queen Victoria's state visit to Scotland in 1842:

'When in 1842 Queen Victoria was to visit Scotland, the Directors [of GSN] made available the *Trident*. Her Majesty, they were informed, had been graciously pleased to decline their offer. However, the 971-ton schooner-rigged paddle steamer accompanied the fleet, and as Her Majesty was about to leave for London she expressed her Royal pleasure to return to England aboard this splendid vessel. Afterwards, she wrote in her diary of the ship: "The accommodation for us was much larger and better than on board the [Royal Yacht] *Royal George* and which was beautifully fitted up." The passage took just 48 hours and Her Majesty remarked that only the *Monarch*, another GSN vessel, had been able to keep up.'

Thomas Brockelbank was a Director of GSN from its inception and was elected Chairman of the Board in November 1828, in which capacity he served until February 1831. From 1827 until his death in 1843 he lived with his family at Westcombe Manor, overlooking the Thames near Greenwich. From his sitting-room windows he could watch his steamers come and go on the river. Brockelbank took the lease for an annual fee of £300. His estate comprised 55 acres of pasture and parkland, and the leasehold was advertised 'as adapted for the reception of a merchant banker or man of opulence'. His vision created the world's first ocean-going steamship company, a company that was to last for nearly 150 years, and whose successors now lie hidden in the P&O Group of companies. His ships, many of which carried some passengers, were affectionately known as the 'navvies' and will long be remembered. His excursion steamers and later motor ships are remembered for the pleasure they gave successive generations of Londoners.

Thomas Brockelbank's *Eagle* (1820) (from a contemporary engraving).

The New Medway Steam Packet Company's *Medway Queen* (1924) seen on the Medway as a new ship, from a photograph taken by Medway Studios of Chatham. *George Robins collection*

GSN was set to be a key player in the Thames passenger and excursion services for the next 142 years, seeing many competitors come and go. Of these, the principal rivals would be the Woolwich Steam Packet Company and its various successors, Belle Steamers, and finally the New Medway Steam Packet Company. GSN was able to protect its excursion services, as it developed a large and for the most part profitable network of passenger and cargo routes, working as far afield as Hamburg in the north and into the Mediterranean in the south. None of the competitors on the Thames routes had such a firm economic buffer against the perpetually low margins on offer and the competitive over-capacity that was to develop on the down-river trade.

GSN and its trading name of Eagle Steamers (reflecting Thomas Brockelbank's original steam packet *Eagle* of 1820) are remembered with affection by Londoners to this day, as well as residents of Southend, Clacton, Margate, Herne Bay and Deal who are old enough to have enjoyed the trip from Tower Pier down to the coastal resorts. They look forward to the annual visits of the *Waverley* and the *Balmoral* (see Chapter 12) in order to relive their childhood days of sailing on the *Royal Sovereign* or the *Queen of the Channel*, 'weather and other circumstances permitting'. Meanwhile that old stalwart the *Medway Queen* lies hapless in her creek while armies of volunteers convert the once sunken hulk back to its former vibrant persona.

2. EXPANSION AND COMPETITION

'...the watermen obstructed the paddle steamers at every turn, with bills introduced in Parliament and more literal and effective obstructions placed in the river. The fact was that the public had been won over, and the steamers thrived. Owners attempted to run "through" services from Richmond to Margate and competition became intense and dangerous. Racing was the cause of more than one fatal accident, yet the popularity of the steamers increased.'

From an article by Norman Fox, *The Illustrated London News*, January 1971

Competition eventually became so fierce that respective owners tried everything above the law, and some things below it, to protect their share of the trade – street fighting and legal injunctions were not uncommon. In addition to steamer operators fighting amongst themselves, the watermen continued their fight against the steamer. The protection afforded the General Steam Navigation Company by its dominance over the Thanet trade and by its general cargo routes provided a significant advantage, and, although the reliability of the newer steamers was greatly improved, they were still expensive units to maintain and operate. In the meantime many of the smaller companies came and went.

In the immediate years after its formation GSN added five new dedicated Thames steamers to its fleet: the *Eclipse* and *Attwood* in 1825, *Columbine* and *Harlequin* in 1826, and the *Ramona* in 1829. Of these the *Harlequin* and *Columbine* are notable as having the most powerful engines, generating 140 nominal horsepower, whereas the engines aboard the *Eclipse* generated only 70. No further vessels were built specifically for Thames service until 1844, although second-hand ships were bought, while the company enjoyed a period of consolidation.* More significantly, GSN was developing services to France and the Lowlands as confidence in trading with Europe slowly increased. This was to provide the company with a firm financial foundation that was able to buffer the varied fortunes of the Thames steamer routes for much of the existence of the company.

The prestige service remained the daily return to Margate, as advertised for the *Eclipse* in the early days of the company:

> 'Every weekday from the Hungerford Market Pier at 7.30am, calling at Old Swan Pier at 7.45am, Tunnel Pier 8.00am and Greenwich 8.30am for Herne Bay and Margate. Directly the steamer starts an excellent plain breakfast can be obtained in the chief cabin, 1/- each, ham eggs etc are plentifully supplied at a trifling additional charge. An excellent band of music is on board.'

The *Eclipse* was scheduled to arrive at Herne Bay at 12.45pm and Margate at 1.30pm. With a 15-minute turn-around at Margate the return arrival at Hungerford Market Pier was at 8.00pm, a service requiring an average speed of more than 12 knots. The *Harlequin* and *Columbine* were the mainstay of a new service from Custom House to Margate and

---

* For a comprehensive history and full fleet list of GSN see my *Birds of the Sea: 150 Years of the General Steam Navigation Company* (2007).

Ramsgate, at 6 shillings return. They were later lengthened and were used in the 1840s for the Calais and Boulogne services and occasionally also to Le Havre. The Boulogne service cost just £1 and allowed passengers 48 hours ashore. Both vessels were active into the 1850s, the *Columbine* being wrecked near Rotterdam in 1856.

The Gravesend Steamboat Company continued to build, and its next vessels were the *Hawk*, which had been delivered in 1826, and the *Greenwich*, which joined the company in 1835. These were smaller ships than the Margate steamers and modestly engined, speed not being a requirement of the daily round trip. However, the *Greenwich* carried a massive 18-pounder gun amidships, the Admiralty's response to the ever-present threat of war.

With the obvious success of GSN, a succession of new companies was created to cater for the ever-expanding demand for the Thames services; the single ship operators were now disappearing very rapidly. Nevertheless, overcrowding was the order of the day. Norman Fox commented in *The Illustrated London News*, 23 January 1971:

> 'The captains did nothing very much to relieve the situation. They collected the fares and there was no method of checking the numbers on board. Eventually, some of the ever-increasing number of companies began employing pursers to collect the fares. The captains objected. Their incomes in danger, they gathered together and formed the Sons of the Thames Company.'

The new ship-owning companies and their years of foundation were:

1829 Milton & Gravesend Steam Packet Company (sold to the Diamond Steam Packet Company in 1835)
Margate & Gravesend Steam Packet Company (The Royal Line)
1833 New Steam Packet Company, later restyled as the Star Steam Packet Company
1834 Woolwich Steam Packet Company
1835 London & Herne Bay Steam Packet Company
London & Westminster Steamboat Company
1838 Iron Steamboat Company (for up-river services to Kew)
1840 Blackwall Railway Company (as ship-owners)
Watermen's Steam Packet Company
1844 Thames Steamboat Company
1845 Eagle Company
1846 Citizen Steamboat Company
Halfpenny Fare Steamers (Dyer's Hall Company)

The Margate & Gravesend Steam Packet Company was taken over by GSN in 1836 in a bid by the larger company to reduce competition. The steamers *William IV*, *Royal George*, *Royal Adelaide* and *Royal William* retained their separate identity as the Royal Line within the GSN umbrella. The Gravesend Steam Packet Company remained the oldest of the established packet companies on the river, together with the Diamond Steam Packet Company and its distinctive black-and-white-diamond-patterned funnels. The Diamond, Star and Woolwich companies all competed for the Gravesend trade, the so-called 'Long Ferry', while the last of the passenger tilt boats to Gravesend was withdrawn in 1834.

The Woolwich boats had the reputation of being the dirtiest packets on the river at one time! They started at Charing Cross (Hungerford Market) and called at Greenwich and Queenhithe initially with only two sailings a day to Gravesend. However, the dirty boats of the river were obviously very successful. They also offered the cheapest fares, and rapid fleet expansion prompted services to be developed beyond to Sheerness and Southend. The company had absorbed the Milton & Gravesend Steam Packet Company as early as 1835, with its four steamers, the *Kent*, *Essex*, *Pearl* and *Fly* easily integrated into the down-river services.

The success of the Woolwich company antagonised the Watermen's Association even further. Interference from its members – for example, accidentally leaving barges in the seaway or assisting spillages from flats reportedly caused by the wash of the steamers – was such that intervention was finally called for. The outcome was the formation of the Watermen's Steam Packet Company in 1840. Within four years a fleet of 12 fast and finely appointed steamers was trying to push the Woolwich company off the board, with schedules that just preceded those of the Woolwich company overtly encouraging races to the next pier. The steamers remained popular even when the South Eastern Railway reached Woolwich in 1847. Fierce and somewhat unhealthy competition ensued for another 15 years when in 1865 the Watermen's company finally conceded defeat and sold out to the Woolwich Steam Packet Company. In truth, the Watermen's Association, wealthy though it was, refused to put any more resources into its packet company. The 'crack' steamers were imaginatively named *Waterman No 1*, *Waterman No 2* and *Waterman No 3* up to *Waterman No 12*, while what should have been *No 13* was given the name *Elphin*, clearly a case of 'unlucky for some'. The Woolwich company subsequently gave the ships birds' names – *Cygnet*, *Ibis*, *Osprey*, etc – in the style later adopted for the GSN nomenclature.

The London & Westminster Steamboat Company ran a fleet of small ships in the London area of the Thames, largely in competition with the Halfpenny Fare Steamers. The London & Westminster ships were all named after flowers – the 'flower boats' – with bell-topped funnels, black with a distinctive white band. The *London Pride* had her original 8-foot-diameter fixed float paddle wheels replaced with the new feathering floats on an 8-foot-diameter wheel in 1849, increasing her speed from just over 10 knots to 13 knots. Many of this generation of ships, built in the 1840s and 1850s, had long careers with a variety of owners on the Thames, including the Citizen Steamboat Company and the Woolwich Steamboat Company. One of them, the *Lotus*, delivered in 1856, survived until 1909, latterly with the London Steamboat Company, the River Thames Steamboat Company and finally the Victoria Steamboat Association, which gave her the name *Lobelia*.

The Gravesend company was reconstituted in 1835 when it employed four ships on the London to Gravesend, Sheerness, Margate and Ramsgate route in competition with GSN. Other competitors were the London & Herne Bay Steam Packet Company with, among other vessels, the popular *Red Rover* and *City of Canterbury*. The *Red Rover* suffered a snapped piston crosshead on passage to London in November 1843, but managed to return to London on one engine, arriving only 3 hours behind schedule. Shortly after she arrived from the builders, the company's *City of Boulogne* was chartered to the South Eastern & Continental Steam Packet Company for the inauguration of the Folkestone to Boulogne service in 1838. She partnered the Diamond Steam Packet Company's *Emerald* of 1835 until the railway company obtained powers to run its own ships in 1844. The *Emerald* ended her days in the ownership of the Licensed Victuallers' Association, running day cruises to Boulogne for the 1855 and 1856 seasons.

On the up-river services, the Iron Steamboat Company and the Citizen Steamboat Company competed for the traffic to Chelsea and Kew. The Citizen fleet takes the second prize for the least

The *Royal William* (1831), seen here in a modern oil painting, was typical of the steamers on the Margate run in the 1830s.

imaginative fleet nomenclature, with the series *Citizen A*, *Citizen B* up to *Citizen S*, with the exception of the letter 'I'. Subsequent owners, the River Thames Steamboat Company and the Victoria Steamboat Association, tended to give the steamers flower names: A became *Azalea*, C *Carnation*, D *Daisy*, F *Fuchsia*, etc.

Unlike on the Clyde, Forth, Humber and Bristol Channel, the railways, except for the brief intervention of both the Blackwall Railway Company and occasional continental services, virtually never operated steamers on the Thames other than cross-river ferries. This was simply because the progressive development of the rail network allowed all the coastal towns to be served directly by rail, eventually leaving a dwindling number of steamer services to the excursionists. Although the North Kent Railway had not greatly eroded traffic to Gravesend, cheap fares on the London, Tilbury & Southend Railway had a serious effect on the Diamond Steam Packet Company, the Star and the Thames companies.

The increasing safety and comfort of the steamers is illustrated by the increased number of excursions that were advertised. One of the first excursions carried out by GSN was by the *Harlequin*, which took 400 passengers round the Nore Light on 9 April 1830. The privately owned steamer *Albion* was chartered on 18 June 1833 by Messrs T. Jones and J. Winsor, again for a trip round the Nore at 5 shillings per head. The price included entertainment by a 'wonderful illusionist', and an 'efficient band':

> 'The promoters trust that the arrangements that they have made for the convenience and conviviality, will meet with the approbation it will be their happiness to merit. The vessel will proceed along the Kent and Essex shores; and from the deck will be visible the various works of art and nature that grace those romantic situations; the Thames Tunnel, that effort of national science and industry, which if completed would be the glory of the world; that splendid palace for decayed seamen, Greenwich Hospital ... and Tilbury Fort, from whence Queen Elizabeth addressed her patriotic partisans, to the ultimate destruction of the Spanish Armada; and so onward to the Nore.'

The withdrawal by GSN from the Margate route is explained by Sarah Palmer in an academic paper in *The Journal of Transport History* (1982):

> 'In 1838 GSN withdrew from Margate as a regular operator, though it continued to provide a service to Ramsgate, leaving the station to the New Margate Company in return for a payment of 9d a passenger in the summer season. In 1841 GSN threatened to "resume the position of the company at Margate" if the agreement was not maintained, and it seems probable that the arrangement continued until 1849, when the GSN purchased the new Margate Company's vessels.'

Iron-hulled steamers slowly replaced the wooden-hulled packets from about 1840, again enhancing the safety and integrity of the vessels. In these days, before the engine room telegraph had been invented, a 'call boy', who usually sat on a box by the engine room skylight, was engaged to shout the Captain's orders down to the Engineer below! By 1842 16 steamers ran down from the London piers to the fashionable resort of Gravesend, carrying more than a million passengers a year.

Diamond Packets advertised excursions from London Bridge Wharf to Southend and Sheerness from 1847, calling at the Tunnel, Greenwich, Woolwich, Erith and Gravesend. The company also advertised the *Sons of the Thames* or *Princess Royal* from Hungerford Market Steam Pier (roughly below what is now Charing Cross railway bridge) via London Bridge Wharf to Sheerness, Southend and Chatham.

The Watermen's Company undertook a number of excursions, nearly losing the *Waterman No 10* on an excursion from Dover to Hastings in April 1844. At the time she had been testing the viability of extending services beyond the confines of the Thames to Ostend and Calais.

The year of the London Exhibition, 1851, was a boom year for the steamers. A twin-hulled steamer, the *Gemini*, was built in 1850 to cream off some of the anticipated traffic; alas, despite plush accommodation for 1,000 passengers, she could make no headway against the tide and could gain no steerage. Her trial trip was her last, leaving her inventor and owner £14,000 worse off.

The Thames piers

The provision of a pier or jetty at the initiative of the townspeople ensured the prosperity of seaside towns, as it allowed the paddle steamers to bring Londoners to town to spend their money. Ramsgate recognised this from the start, when the Stone Pier, a new harbour arm, was built in 1815. This sufficed until 1855 when a new jetty was opened, running at right angles to the shore end of the harbour arm and some 1,240 feet in length. Extended in 1877, it was given a landing stage to accommodate up to three large steamers at a time.

An exception was the pier at Herne Bay, which was built for a quite different reason. The timber pier, some 3,700 feet long, was completed in 1833, and was opened for the conveyance of the mail from Dover to London, coming by mail coach to Herne Bay then transhipped by steamer to London to avoid the footpads on the outskirts of the city. Sadly, the town lost its pier in 1863 when the decking became too rotten and dangerous for traffic. An iron pier of just 320 feet in length was opened in 1873, and it was against this structure that the *Glen Rosa* berthed at high tide alongside a barge with a ladder from the barge to the deck of the pier in 1891 (see Chapter 4). Five years later, Herne Bay Pier was extended into deep water and the steamers once again became a regular feature. Interestingly the deck timbers were laid crosswise, a feature that set children vibrating in their prams as they were wheeled towards the shore!

Deal possessed a wooden pier until plans to replace it with an iron pier were laid down in 1861. The new pier was 1,000 feet long and featured a promenade walkway. It remained in use by the steamers from London and Dover until the outbreak of war in 1914, and thereafter was open to promenaders, although corrosion had made it unsuitable for steamer traffic. It was demolished after the Second World War. The present concrete pier was opened in 1957, complete with spring piling at the pier head to facilitate berthing in what are exposed seas. The GSN motor ships used this pier until their demise in the 1960s.

At Dover the steamers used the short Promenade Pier until the Prince of Wales Pier opened in 1902. However, the *Conqueror* continued to use the Promenade Pier under the West Cliff until the First World War (see Chapter 5).

The *Glen Rosa* (1877) off Brighton wearing the white Campbell funnel.

The story of Southend Pier is told by H. Collard Stone in an article that first appeared in *Paddle Wheels* in August 1971:

> 'The town's people of Southend, with a full mile of black Thames silt before water is reached at low tide, must have looked with envy on the Burgesses of Margate, watching the steamboats passing along the fairway to and from their town. Southend's population at that time was no more than a few hundred people living close to the sea shore at the south end of the ancient monastic village of Prittlewell, its church and priory nearly a mile inland, hence the name South End became established.
>
> During the Regency period it had received some Royal patronage as a watering place; a lone terrace of fine houses, built in the style of the period, remains to the present day, then quite by themselves on the cliff, with just fishermen's cottages along the shore. Now the first *Eagle* was proudly sailing to Margate, and the GSN had entered the field, so it was not surprising that the local landowners promoted a Bill in 1829 that, after receiving the Royal Assent, established the Pier Company.
>
> The first section of the pier, some 1,500 feet in length, was opened in 1830 and was eventually continued until it extended to about half a mile from the shore. As the tide receded beyond this point, passengers desiring to embark had to proceed from here on foot or by cart along a hard-way of shingle for a further quarter of a mile, where they were faced by a stretch of water over which they had to be ferried in small boats to the pier head. This was at first an old vessel about 100 feet in length, later replaced by a structure on piles called the Mount. In spite of its inconvenience a daily service of steamboats from London was soon in operation.'

The pier was extended in 1846 to one mile and a quarter. It was constructed entirely of wood and included a tramway drawn by two horses. This structure served the steamers until 1875, when the pier was acquired for just £10,000 by the Southend Local Board, which immediately laid a project before Parliament to build a new iron pier. This was opened in 1889, a mile and a quarter long with an electric tramway and a pier pavilion at the shore end. It cost £69,000, and in 1898 a further £21,000 was invested in a 1,500-foot-long extension providing berths for three steamers and space for the lifeboat station. Additional berths were added in the 1930s when the Prince George extension was built. In the war years that followed, the pier head became an important staging post for the Admiralty and was the control centre for all North Sea convoys.

With the help of the steamers and the arrival of the railway the population of Southend grew to 7,000 by 1870. When established as a County Borough in 1908 its population was 77,000.

Clacton's pier preceded the town almost completely. Built by the engineer who had built the Eastern Union Railway, Peter Bruff, the pier was opened on 18 July 1871 with the first sailing of the *Queen of the Orwell*. A contemporary account states:

> 'PS *Queen of the Orwell* regularly sailing between London and Harwich left Harwich on this occasion with Mr Bruff aboard in company with people interested in coastal development. Whilst the ship prepared to berth, Bruff pointed to a gap in the cliff with only green fields above it, and exclaimed: that is the land on which you can build the town.'

The pier was extended in 1877 so that ships could berth at all states of the tide. H. Collard Stone picks up the story after the London, Woolwich & Clacton-on-Sea Steamship Company had been established:

> 'Clacton at once continued to thrive, and so did their steamers. As their number increased a wider area was covered by them, especially along the East Coast,

Above This famous, but contrived, picture of Southend Pier graced Eagle Steamers publications in the 1950s, and shows the *Royal Sovereign* (1949) and *Royal Daffodil* (1939) alongside and the *Queen of the Channel* (1948), wearing the flag of the New Medway Steam Packet Company on her funnel, in the foreground.

Below The *Royal Eagle* and the *Queen of Thanet* at Margate Pier in the 1930s.

running from London as far as Great Yarmouth. The older resort of Walton-on-the-Naze, a few miles further along the Essex coast, extended its own short pier into deep water so that the steamers could call there. In fact three berths were provided at its pier head, becoming as busy as a railway junction, through its being midway between London and Yarmouth, and was as far as the return journey in both directions could be done in the day. In addition it served the steamboats coming down the River Orwell from Ipswich, which made it the interchanging pier for the East Coast.

At the turn of the century [1900] there were no coastal piers after Walton, the entire Suffolk coast being without them. By then the Clacton steamers had been reconstituted as the Coast Development Corporation, [and it was this company that was] eventually [responsible for] building them. The first in 1900 was at Southwold, a wooden structure similar in design and length to Clacton's, the second in 1903 towards the southern end of Lowestoft seafront, being given the name of Claremont Pier, quite similar, and the third in 1905 on Felixstowe seafront. While similar to the others, due to shallow water inshore [the Felixstowe pier] was three-quarters of a mile in length, having an electric railway running down it.'

Before the new Suffolk piers had been constructed the Yarmouth steamer slowed opposite the respective resorts so that passengers who so wished could be taken off in small boats. An advertisement in the *Lowestoft Journal* for June 1898 assigns this duty locally to the two beach yawls *Courage sans Pier* and *Star of the East*.

Mention should also be made of Tower Pier. Completed only in 1929, this became the home of most of the steamers. The Pool of London had by then become very congested, and some operators had to resort to ferrying their passengers out to the steamers in the river, while others terminated at Greenwich. The opening of this dedicated facility was essential to the continuation of services from London city centre between the wars.

In 1853 a group of Margate businessmen set about raising the profile of the town by commissioning the very first iron pier. Designed by Eugenius Birch, it incorporated iron piles that were screwed into the ground and a style that reflected the designer's earlier experience working in India. The pier withstood the ravages of winter storms until it was eventually destroyed in 1878. Earlier piers were built with tall wooden piles driven into the seabed, with a flimsy wooden deck suspended from chains hung from the tops of the piles.

Cheap railway fares to Gravesend offered by the North Kent Railway and to Southend by the London, Tilbury & Southend Railway put the Star Company, the Thames Company and the Diamond Steam Packet Company out of business by 1855. At the demise of their owners, the Diamond steamers *Topaz*, *Ruby*, *Sapphire* and *Diamond* were bought by GSN for £4,252 10s.

The seaside was becoming hugely fashionable and people were convinced of the health-giving properties of a stiff ozone-filled breeze and even a dip in the sea. Although the prospect of a day out of town sailing down the river was ever appealing to Londoners, the condition of the river above Gravesend was not in the least pleasant. Each house had its own cess pit below the ground floor, which would periodically be emptied and taken away for disposal or would more likely overflow into gullies that eventually flowed down to the Thames. Three separate cholera outbreaks had claimed several thousand lives over the years. Matters finally came to a head in the summer of 1858 when 'The Great Stink' occurred. Just as the *Great Eastern* was being fitted out down river, 'The Great Stink' saw thousands flee the city, leaving Parliament, which was obliged to remain in session, hiding behind drapes soaked in chloride of lime at the windows. It was then that Joseph Bazalgette was commissioned to start to engineer and develop the London sewage system, complete with his famous aqueduct to discharge the sewage to the river below Woolwich. But the river was set to remain a toxic brew for some time to come, and those unfortunate enough to fall into it risked asphyxiation rather than drowning!

Throughout the mid-19th century, the Woolwich Steam Packet Company slowly became a very important player on the Thames, vying even with the aloof and secure operations of GSN. Burtt (1949) reports:

> 'As river traffic became more popular and the railways had not yet obtained the monopoly of the traffic on both sides of the river, the services were extended to Southend and Sheerness. In 1865 the Woolwich Company amalgamated with the Iron, Citizen and Westminster companies and in 1871 with the Watermen's Steam Packet Company, and all their piers were brought into the Woolwich fold. This combined grouping secured for the Woolwich Company a monopoly of the Thames passenger traffic from Kew and Richmond up the river down to Southend and Sheerness at the mouth.'

Indeed, from 1865 the Woolwich Steam Packet Company was running the steamers *Queen of the Thames* and *Queen of the Orwell* from London Bridge daily to Ipswich.

It was at this time that the saloon steamer, first developed on the Clyde, arrived on the Thames, all previous steamers being of the traditional flush deck design. Representations were made by the Scottish Shipbuilders' Association in 1861 that the volume of the deck saloons erected solely for the shelter of passengers on river steamers should not be included in their tonnage. The Board of Trade agreed to this request, although the decision was reversed in later years.

The blockade-runner *Alexandra* had been built at Port Glasgow and equipped with state-of-the-art diagonal oscillating engines. Before she could take up service for the Confederate Army the American Civil War had ended, and in 1865 she was sold to the newly formed Saloon Steam Packet Company, London, for service between London Bridge and Gravesend. Becoming the saloon steamer *Alexandra*, she was then the largest, and probably the best appointed, steamer on the river, at 279 tons gross. Unsurprisingly she eventually found herself under the colours of the Woolwich Company, from the 1875 season onwards.

3. THE 'HAPHAZARD OPERATION OF ILL-EQUIPPED STEAMERS'

A number of Clyde steamers found their way into the Watermen's, later the Woolwich and later still the London Steamboat Company. Four steamers, the *Ardencaple*, *Ardgowan*, *Leven* and *Craigrownie*, were bought by the Woolwich company and given 'Duke' names. The *Kyles* and *Bute*, built in 1865 for the Wemyss Bay Railway Company, had been sold in 1867 to the Watermen's company, thence to the Woolwich company. The Watermen's company had planned to develop excursion services with these relatively large vessels, even though their original owners had been unable to make them pay their way on the Clyde.

The Wemyss Bay Railway Company had been dissatisfied with the performance of the *Kyles* and *Bute* and was concerned with the weak construction of the vessels, which included iron plates that were only three-sixteenths of an inch thick. The Watermen's company compounded the weakness by adding deck saloons with a Promenade Deck above, to give them a licensed passenger complement of nearly 1,000 down river to Gravesend and just under 500 beyond. But the sisters were a great favourite with the public and, when taken over by the Woolwich company, the *Kyles* was renamed *Albert Edward* and the *Bute* the *Princess Alice*. Indeed, it was the *Princess Alice* that was used to convey the Shah of Persia around London Docks in 1873.

Excursions were also advertised by train and ship through Folkestone, and sometimes Dover, by the South Eastern Railway and the London, Chatham & Dover Railway respectively. The very first day excursion to Boulogne took place on 24 June 1843, four days before the new South Eastern Railway service to Folkestone was opened to the public. The crossing was undertaken by the wooden-hulled *Waterwitch*, chartered from GSN for the day, and originally built for the Humber Steamship Company in 1835. Eric Harrison described the event in an article that first appeared in *Sea Breezes* in September 1967:

> 'Leaving London Bridge at 6.00am the special train called at five stations before reaching Folkestone at 8.40am. Passengers included Directors, Members of Parliament and "certain gentlemen interested in scientific promotion". The *Waterwitch* was able to cast off about 9.15am. By 12.30pm all passengers were ashore at Boulogne where the authorities were astounded to receive copies of the same day's London newspapers.
>
> As was customary at Victorian transport occasions, the company partook of a "delectable collation" served in a saloon at the Baths. Toasts were given, speeches made, and goodwill radiated generally. After luncheon visitors returned to the steamer, "escorted by a gazing and cheering multitude" to quote from the newspaper report. Leaving Boulogne at 2.40pm, the *Waterwitch* made Folkestone Harbour by 6.30pm. Presumably an adverse tide was encountered. At 10.05pm the train was in London, so the round trip had been accomplished in the incredible time of 16 hours.'

By the 1860s the South Eastern Railway undertook innumerable seasonal excursions including fortnightly cheap trips to Boulogne and hour-long coastal cruises taken by the inbound steamer. On 29 July 1867 the South Eastern Railway's cross-Channel steamer *Prince Ernest* took the Tradesmen's Annual Outing to Boulogne, the 240 excursionists being 'accompanied by May and Fidge's Quadrille band'.

Campbell connections

The connection between Clyde and Thames steamers is a thread that can be followed throughout the history of the London excursion ships. Many of the Thames steamers were, of course, ordered from Clydeside shipbuilders, but there were many Clyde steamers that found their way to the Thames through the second-hand market. Of these, the steamers associated with the Campbell family of Kilmun, who moved their enterprise to the Bristol Channel in the late 1880s as the foundation of the famous White Funnel Steamers of P. & A. Campbell, are some of the more interesting.

In 1866 the Greenock & Helensburgh Steamboat Company built four steamers for the Gareloch trade, in which they competed for traffic with the Campbell steamers. Of these, the *Ardencaple* was bought by Campbells in 1869 prior to the delivery of her replacement, the *Craigrownie*. Shortly after that Bob Campbell joined forces with Hugh Keith & Company, and with capital from the new partner Campbell was able to buy out his competitors. The deal included the sisters *Ardencaple*, *Leven* and *Ardgowan*, and the almost brand-new *Craigrownie*, the erstwhile replacement for the *Ardencaple*. It was these four ships that the Campbell and Keith partnership sold in the winter of 1875/76 to the London Steamboat Company, which gave them their 'Duke' names.

The tenure of the *Ardencaple* and *Craigrownie* in the Campbell fleet reads like a catalogue of disaster, and Campbell was probably pleased to see them eventually head south. First, in June 1871, the *Ardencaple* was struck by a new steamer completing her trials, and had to be beached to avoid loss. Then in May 1873 the *Craigrownie*, under the command of Alexander Campbell, was struck by the steamer *Hero* at Garelochhead. This time the *Hero* was beached in a sinking condition and the *Craigrownie* was able to return both steamers' complement of passengers to Port Glasgow.

Less fortunate was the incident in December 1873 when the *Craigrownie* was sunk in collision with a freighter off Greenock. Happily, all her passengers were able to transfer to the cargo ship, while Captain Alexander Campbell and three crew members stayed unsuccessfully with the *Craigrownie* in an attempt to beach her before she sank. She was later raised and put back into service. Then, during the Glasgow Fair Fortnight in 1875, the *Ardencaple* was struck in mid-channel at Govan. Although the ship ended facing the wrong way with bows stuck in the mud, there were no injures. Finally, in August 1875 the *Craigrownie* was in collision as she and another steamer attempted to leave Greenock at the same time.

Once on the Thames, the *Ardencaple* and *Leven*, respectively renamed the *Duke of Connaught* and *Duke of Teck*, performed impeccably until withdrawn in 1889. The *Ardgowan* and *Craigrownie*, respectively the Thames steamers *Duke of Cambridge* and *Duke of Edinburgh*, were withdrawn in 1898 after spending their last few years in the service of the Victoria Steamboat Association (see Chapter 4).

Two further Clyde steamers, the *Glen Rosa* and the *Bonnie Doon*, were to find their way into Thames service, and later complete the link with the Campbell company by subsequently joining the P. & A. Campbell fleet towards the end of their careers (see Chapter 4). The Campbell link continues to 1939/40, when its new turbine steamer *Empress Queen* was built to almost the same hull design as the GSN steamer *Queen of the Channel* (see Chapter 9). The hull of the *Queen of the Channel*, although a motor ship, was modelled on the Clyde steamer *Queen Mary*, built in 1933 for John Williamson, and later a fleet member of the Caledonian Steam Packet Company. The final Thames link with P. & A. Campbell was the highly unsuccessful charter of the little GSN-owned motor ship, the *Crested Eagle*, for use on the South Coast in 1957 (see Chapter 11).

The *Waterwitch* (1835) ran the first day excursion to Boulogne for the South Eastern Railway. *DP World P&O Heritage Collection*

The last outing of the year was that of the Druid's Friendly Society, during which May and Fidge's Quadrille band 'enlivened the voyage with harmonious strains'.

Eric Harrison described a later excursion from Folkestone that never actually took place:

> 'Despite the Franco-Prussian War, the ship [*Albert Edward*] was booked to make a special day excursion to Boulogne on 8 August 1870, but to the great disappointment of a huge crowd which arrived by rail from country districts the excursion was cancelled at the last moment. The authorities at Boulogne, because of mounting war losses, were instructed to ask for all travellers to have passports, yet no staff was available to examine them, and willy nilly, they had to call off the trip.'

Indeed, by the early 1880s the South Eastern Railway's *Albert Edward*, which had been built by Samuda Brothers on the Thames in 1862, was reduced to relief steamer and seasonal excursion boat. The excursions included trips to Deal and Broadstairs (especially during the regattas) and coastal cruises to Dungeness and beyond, some of which were taken by the slightly younger cross-Channel steamer *Napoleon III*. The *Napoleon III* was also famed for her moonlit coastal cruises, but she also carried out a number of cross-Channel excursions, being for many years the preferred paddler for the Oddfellows annual outing to Boulogne.

The GSN Thames-based steamers, meanwhile, were enjoying an expansive phase. A number of second-hand steamers had been bought for the trade, and in 1844 the three-year-old *Little Western* was acquired for the Margate station. With a gilded serpent adorning her bows and cabins described as sumptuous and luxurious, she was surely an important asset for attracting excursionists. She was joined in 1848 by the *Albion*, and in 1849 GSN bought the *Prince of Wales* from the Margate Steam Packet Company. Given new boilers and engines, equipped now with feathering floats, the *Prince of Wales* was completely refitted, ready to share Margate and Ramsgate duties with the *Little Western*. Four steamers from the defunct Diamond Steam Packet Company had also joined the GSN fleet between 1853 and 1855 specifically to serve the Gravesend and Southend routes (see Chapter 2).

Table 2: The early Thames steamships of the General Steam Navigation Company (after Burtt, 1949)

Name	Built	Year acquired	Year displaced	Gross tons	Length (ft)	Breadth (ft)	Nominal hp
Earl of Liverpool	1823	1824		262	128	20	100
Lord Melville	1822	1824	1845[1]	116 net	130	21	70
Royal Sovereign	1822	1824		220	135	19	100
City of London	1824	1824		213	126	19	30
Victory	1818	1824		160			40
Eclipse	1821	1825		88	104	17	70
Attwood	1825	1825		310	147	20	100
Columbine	1826	1826	1855	393	158	25	140
Harlequin	1825	1826	1856	315	138	22	140
Ramona	1828	1829		356	149	22	100
Little Western[2]	1841	1843	1876	431	198	25	180
Albion[3]	1848	1848	1887	338	174	23	125
Prince of Wales	1843	1849	1880	429	180	22	136
Eagle	1853	1856	1888	325	200	24	130
Sir Walter Raleigh	1858	1862	1891	239	169	21	100
Hilda	1862	1869	1889	428	225	24	220
Hoboken	1873	1877	1897	413	222	23	200

[1] The wooden-hulled ships were generally hulked and the year of abandonment left unrecorded, whereas the iron ships were sold for scrap. The *Columbine* was lost off Rotterdam

[2] Composite iron and wood hull

[3] The first iron-hulled steamer in the GSN Thames fleet

Below **The General Steam Navigation Company's continental steamer the *Britannia* (1835).** *DP World P&O Heritage Collection*

Right **Other GSN continental steamers: (*top to bottom*) the *Lapwing* (1879), *Hirondelle* (1890) and *Groningen* (1928).**

SANDPIPER

Left, top to bottom **The GSN continental steamers *Drake* (1938), *Sheldrake* (1956) and *Sandpiper* (1957).**

A new *Eagle*, built originally for Mr G. W. Morris, was bought into the fleet at the age of three in 1856, and was licensed to carry 466 passengers as far as Dover. Although only a flush deck ship, she made a fine sight with her golden eagle figurehead and scrollwork at the bow, white paddle box and red floats and dark blue lifeboats. More second-hand tonnage, the *Sir Walter Raleigh*, was acquired in 1862, and the *Hilda* in 1868. The latter had been built in 1862 for the South Eastern Railway as the *Eugénie*, named after the French Empress, and operated between Folkestone and Boulogne. In 1864 she was sold to the Confederate Army as the blockade-runner *Cornubia*. Although set on fire by her crew to avoid capture by the Federal Navy, she was brought back across the Atlantic, reboilered and refitted to become the only two-funnelled steamer then in the GSN fleet. In 1867 GSN commenced excursions to Essex piers and in 1867 extended the service to Lowestoft.

The crowning glory was the acquisition of the saloon steamer *Hoboken*. She was built in 1873 by Napier & Son at Glasgow for the German Adler Line for use as a tender on the River Elbe. When the Adler Line was taken over by HAPAG in 1875, the *Hoboken*, together with several other vessels, was found to be surplus to requirements and was put on the sale list. GSN bought her and she arrived in the Thames in time for the 1877 season. This fine ship was modern in every way and was equipped with the newly developed diagonal compound engines. Her Promenade Deck was continuous from the foremast nearly to the stern, but there were open alleyways either side of the saloon on the Main Deck.

The *Hoboken* helped on the Margate duties in tandem with the *Hilda* and the *Eagle*. Often three ships were required, one of which was known as the 'Husbands' boat', leaving London after Saturday morning work was over, and allowing the husbands to join their families at the seaside for at least part of the weekend. Some runs included an extension to Deal, staying overnight at Margate, and returning to London the next day. Occasional additional services were made with GSN steamers normally employed on the continental routes, and the *Concordia*, *Seine* and *Moselle* were all regular visitors to Margate.

Given the strength of GSN on the Thanet routes and its ability to bring in steamers from its continental trades at short notice, it was not surprising that the Woolwich company, strong as it was perceived to be, sought to consolidate further. And so it was that, in 1875, the London Steamboat Company was formed to take over the assets of the Woolwich company, including its associate companies, the Watermen's, Iron and Citizen companies, and assist with mergers with lesser companies to create a fleet totalling 70 vessels trading under one banner. Many of the

The *Hoboken* (1873) was an early example of the saloon steamer (from a modern oil painting).

ships were, however, up-river steamers plying solely between Woolwich and Richmond. The estuarial vessels in the fleet were:

The Ipswich steamers: *Queen of the Orwell*, *Queen of the Thames*, *Duke of Connaught* (ex-*Ardencaple*), *Duke of Cambridge* (ex-*Ardgowan*), *Duke of Teck** (ex-*Leven*) and *Duke of Edinburgh* (ex-*Craigrownie*)
The Gravesend and Sheerness steamers: *Albert Edward*, *Princess Alice* and *Alexandra*
The Southend steamers: *Sea Swallow*, *Petrel* and *Oread*.

In addition, the *Éclair* was purchased with the assets of J. F. d'Oyly in 1877 to operate general excursion duties for the company. Three up-river steamers were also acquired from two other small operators the previous winter.

Occasional attempts were made to break into the excursion trade by new companies. The *Fairy Queen* was built for one such company in 1860, and designed for the Ramsgate to Dover excursion traffic, but lasted just one season. She was sold in order to settle the shipbuilder's bill, and was duly sent off to her new owners in Palermo. Her master, both while the ship was based at Ramsgate and for her delivery voyage to Sicily, was Captain Frederick Knight.

There remained only one significant independent operator on the Thames estuary other than the London Steamboat Company and GSN, and that was the Medway Steam Packet Company, incorporated in 1837 to connect Chatham and Sheerness. In 1876 the company operated the small wooden-hulled steamers *City of Rochester*, built entirely of mahogany in 1849, the *Alma* of 1855 and the *Lady of Lorne* of 1871. They were employed on services between Chatham, Sheerness and Southend. Charles Dance described the trio in an article that first appeared in *Sea Breezes* in September 1978:

> 'In these ships the engine room was reached through a small square hatch in the deck. The machinery consisted of two cylinder jet condensing oscillating engines taking steam straight from the boiler through two steam pipes, which meant two throttle valves and two reversing levers to handle. The engines were coupled so that one could not be disconnected from the other. The boilers had two furnaces, and in one steamer the stoker lost his life when his fire shovel was caught in the machinery in the confined space. The boilers worked at a pressure of 20psi. These early paddle steamers had black hulls and funnels, buff upperworks and white paddle boxes, carrying the ship's name in blue letters.'

Thus there were three main companies now in operation and each had a niche area: GSN served the southern estuary Thanet ports; the London Steamboat Company served the northern estuary ports as far as Ipswich; and the Medway Steam Packet Company served its Medway and cross-Thames function. So buoyant had business become that by 1878 the London company was able to add three new vessels to its down-river fleet, the *Osprey*, *Princess Mary* and *Princess of Wales*, as well as the sisters *Bridegroom* and *Wedding Ring* as replacements for earlier namesakes on the up-river Richmond service. However, the cosy division of routes between the three key operators was not to last, as fate was about to deal a mortal blow.

The disaster that befell the *Princess Alice* at Beckton on Tuesday 3 September 1878 changed the river passenger trade for ever. The tragedy took place in the growing dusk, while the band played on the afterdeck and passengers relaxed on their homeward journey after a long day at the coast. Rather than retell the story of the tragedy, the following passage is offered; written by T. E. Hughes, it first appeared in *Sea Breezes* in October 1978:

> 'When in the early evening the *Princess Alice* left Sheerness to begin her homeward voyage, it was estimated she was carrying 487 passengers. This total was considerably increased when she called at Gravesend at 1900 hours where over 250 excursionists embarked. They included 183 passengers who

* Named after Prince Francis, First Duke of Teck, who married Princess Mary Adelaide of Cambridge, whose daughter married Prince George, later King George V, and who then became Queen Mary.

had spent the day at the popular Rosherville Gardens. The exact total was never determined as no account was taken of the number of children accompanying their parents. It was not easy to do so. Children under six years of age travelled free while those under 12 counted as half an adult.

But in the gathering dusk of that lovely September evening as the *Princess Alice* left Gravesend, her last place of call, nobody was worried about the possibility that the ship was overcrowded. On deck a band played popular tunes while the children danced and adults joined lustily in the choruses. All was gaiety and merriment. They were in the safe hands of Captain William Grinstead, popular master of a popular ship. With him on the bridge were the First Mate, Lang, and John Eyres at the wheel, acting as helmsman; Hopgood, with the Master's consent, had left the ship at Gravesend.'

Hopgood was the regular helmsman and Captain Grinstead had been assured that his replacement by John Eyres, apparently Hopgood's brother-in-law, for the journey up river from Gravesend was in order. It turns out that Eyres had never previously handled a ship of this size on the river, and Captain Grinstead's acceptance of the replacement helmsman reflects the haphazard organisation of the river steamers at that time.

Just after eight in the evening the lights of Woolwich came into view as the *Princess Alice* approached Tripcock Point. Beyond the bend in the river the 1,370-gross-tons steamer *Bywell Castle* was heading downstream, making the most of the ebb tide. Hughes's narrative continues:

'As the big screw-propelled collier neared Tripcock Point, her Trinity House pilot, Captain Dix, taking the ship down river as far as Gravesend, observed the red port light of the *Princess Alice*. There was nothing unusual about this. Dix assumed, quite correctly, that the *Princess Alice* was about to cross the river to

The *Princess Alice* (1865) disaster from a contemporary etching. *The Illustrated London News*

the north bank, in this way taking advantage of the slacker water. Unfortunately, as the pleasure steamer rounded the point she encountered the full force of the fast ebbing tide, which swept her relentlessly towards the opposite bank to the dismay and consternation of Acting Helmsman John Eyres. Realising the danger, Captain Grinstead ordered Eyres to hold his starboard helm, which, had he been able to do so, would have taken the *Princess Alice* safely round the point.

But the force of the tide proved too strong for Eyres. Virtually out of control, the *Princess Alice* continued on her course until she reached slacker water near the shore. It was only then that she was able to answer her helm, which in the position she was now in proved a fatal mistake, taking her right into the path of the *Bywell Castle*, on board which Captain Dix, in a frantic attempt to avert a collision, rang down "Stop Engines". It was too late. Within seconds, the collier, towering some 20 feet above the doomed pleasure steamer, struck the *Princess Alice* just forward of her starboard paddle box, cutting some 14 feet through her side and opening up her engine room, which immediately began to flood. Scores of passengers were hurled into the river by the force of the impact, while others hysterically jumped overboard in the vague hope of saving themselves.'

Sadly many of the passengers died, choking and vomiting in the toxic waters rather than drowning (both the northern and southern city sewage outfalls discharged into the Thames nearby). Many of the women lost that day would not have assisted their plight in the water by wearing their voluminous Victorian clothing. Only 69 passengers were saved, and many of the dead were never recovered. The body of the master, Captain Grinstead, was found five days later on the mud downstream. A memorial to the dead, a Celtic cross, stands to this day in Woolwich Cemetery.

Whether the weak construction of the ship contributed to the disaster remains unknown. The subsequent Inquiry put the blame on the helmsman of the *Princess Alice*, allegedly misinterpreting the oncoming lights of the collier in the growing dusk. The Inquiry raised a number of questions about safety and the hitherto 'haphazard operation of ill-equipped steamers', and the steamer operators were collectively taken to task. Ironically, the *Bywell Castle*, which had been sailing in ballast after a refit at Millwall, was listed missing in January 1883, lost with all hands in the Bay of Biscay. Her normal route was from Newcastle, with bunker coal for the liners to take on board at Alexandria, returning to England with cotton seed.

The result of the tragedy was immediate. Passenger traffic on the Thames took a sudden down-turn, and passengers no longer thronged to the city piers to board the steamers. By 1884 the London Steamboat Company was all but bankrupt, and its assets were put up for sale. The competitive price war between the new steam-driven District Railway and the Road Car Company and the General Omnibus Company certainly aggravated the situation with loss of traffic between the North Bank piers. At an auction in December various parts of the company were sold, but the rump of the steamer operations went to a newly formed enterprise named the River Thames Steamboat Company. Many of the older, obsolete, wooden-hulled river steamers were sold for the price of their recoverable parts.

GSN fared better, being insulated from the down-turn in the Thames trade by income from its continental steamer network. Nonetheless, no new steamers were bought new or second-hand from the commissioning of the saloon steamer *Hoboken* in 1873 until 1887, and then only because a newly established company was rumoured to be placing new luxury steamers into the Thames excursion trade (see Chapter 4).

Given this sad state of affairs, it is perhaps surprising that an innovative screw steamer, the *Express*, with high-pressure (400psi) boilers, was introduced to the Thames excursion trade under the ownership of Loftus Perkins. The *Express* ran daily from Blackwall to Gravesend, Southend, Sheerness and around the Nore Light in the summer season. She had six watertight compartments, a response to the *Princess Alice* disaster. The high-pressure engines gave her a clear advantage on fuel economy, but she was really too slow to compete with the paddlers and in 1889 was sold to Norwegian owners, who promptly gave her new engines.

4. THE START OF THE HALCYON DAYS

The failure of the London Steamboat Company in 1884 was a severe blow to Thames shipping interests. However, before its demise it acquired two rather interesting vessels that it bought from the Thames & Channel Steamship Company in 1883. These were the steamers *Vale of Clwyd* and *Glen Rosa*, both of which had retained their original names while on Thames duties. The Thames & Channel company was partly in competition with the London Steamboat Company, while some routes were jointly marketed by the two companies.

The iron-hulled paddle steamer *Vale of Clwyd* was built on the Clyde in 1865 for R. W. Preston for service between Liverpool and Rhyl, the latter town situated at the mouth of the Clwyd River in North Wales. After only one season she was sold to Seath & Steele for that company's Glasgow to Ayr service, later seeing service on the Campbell & Gillies Wemyss Bay service. Throughout her Scottish years she was always referred to verbally and in advertisements as the 'Vale of Clyde'. In 1881 she moved south and started work on excursions from the Thanet ports to Dunkirk, Calais and Boulogne.

She was joined by the *Glen Rosa*, a ship reputedly capable of 21 knots. This steamer had been built in 1877 for the small independent company, Shearer Brothers & Ritchie, and placed on the Glasgow to Arran route via Bute, calling at both Rothesay and Kilchattan Bay. The failure of Shearer Brothers presented an opportunity for the London & Channel Steamship Company to acquire her. Whereas the *Vale of Clwyd* was scrapped in 1888, the *Glen Rosa* survived the Great War, although she was last used on the Thames in 1893, latterly with the Victoria Steamboat Association.

Among the main claims to fame of the *Glen Rosa* were the inauguration of the single-day round trip to Clacton, occasional Clacton to Margate excursions, and trips from Margate to Boulogne, Calais or Dunkirk. The *Glen Rosa* also reintroduced calls at Herne Bay, when in 1891 a barge was used as a landing stage at the pier head. Steamers brought people and people brought money, as H. Collard Stone reported in *Paddle Wheels*, No 37, 1969:

> 'A glowing account of the trip and its reception by the people of Herne Bay appeared in the *Herne Bay Star*, in which it is stated – "the town was en fete on Saturday last, when for the first time for very many years, a pleasure steamer, the *Glen Rosa*, made a trip from London Bridge to Herne Bay, with some 220 persons aboard. As the vessel came alongside she was received with a salute fired from the beach and to which she responded." Apparently the trip was repeated on the two subsequent days, and again on a number of consecutive dates ... which suggests coincidence with Spring Tides, when inshore landing could only have been possible. The return fare was 5/-, calls being made at Blackwall, Greenwich, Woolwich, Gravesend and Southend.'

The year 1885 saw the newly formed River Thames Steamboat Company take over the bankrupt London Steamboat Company. But the new company soon also ran out of money as prospective passengers still dwelled on the *Princess Alice* disaster. The River Thames Steamboat Company had received a cash injection of £67,000 from its investors on formation, but as early as June 1886 the whole lot was put up for sale:

'Messrs Fuller, Horsey, Sons & Casell are instructed by the Directors of the River Thames Steamboat Company to offer for sale by tender, as a going concern, in one lot, on Tuesday, 1 June 1886, the business and the whole of the valuable properties of the company comprising:
...[Items 1-5 wharves, piers and property]...
Item 6. The fleet of vessels, consisting of 57 paddle wheel steam vessels adapted for the passenger service of the Thames between London and Hampton Court on the up-river service and below bridge to Greenwich, Woolwich, Gravesend, Sheerness, Southend, Clacton-on-Sea and Harwich. 39 of these vessels have or will have Board of Trade certificates, and include the fast and favourite vessel, the *Glen Rosa* on the Clacton service, the *Alexandra, Albert Edward, Duke of Edinburgh* and *Queen of the Orwell* on the Gravesend, Southend and Sheerness line; and the *Rosalind, Celia* and *Orlando*, built by Sir W. Armstrong Mitchell & Co in 1855, and fitted with all recent improvements for light draft navigation; and there are 18 vessels laid up in the docks and yards...'

There were no takers and the company was forced to struggle on. The first thing to happen was the cessation of the longer routes to Southend and Clacton-on-Sea, leaving a series of unpaid pier dues in its wake. While many of the smaller and older wooden hulled up-river steamers were sold for scrap or left as hulks, some of the down-river fleet was sacrificed as well. Among the larger ships to go were the *Princess of Wales*, which was sold for further service as the *Bembridge* for the Southsea & Ventnor Steamship Company in 1886, and the *Albert Edward*, sister to the ill-fated *Princess Alice*, together with the *Éclair* and *Vale of Clwyd*, which were all sold for scrap in 1888. In September 1889 the *Alexandra* sank under London Bridge, and was later raised and broken up.

To its credit, the River Thames Steamboat Company did introduce a number of small steamers to the up-river services, including the *Cardinal Wolsey* and the slightly smaller trio of *The Shah*, *Kaiser* and *H. M. Stanley*, all built at London in 1889. Happily, in 1890 a new injection of cash was identified and the assets and goodwill of the River Thames Steamboat Company became the property of the Victoria Steamboat Association. The up-river fleet was partly dispersed and a much reduced pier-to-pier service was left in place. However, three new river steamers were built in 1891, the *Bismarck, Empress Frederick* and *The Mermaid*, the latter for the London piers to Rosherville Gardens service. *The Mermaid* was sold to the Rosherville Pier & Steam Packet Company in 1912 for short-duration excursions and feeder services to the pleasure gardens. She was sold in 1916 for use on the Humber ferry, ending her days in the 1920s working in Ireland.

The sea-going fleet, however, was set to flourish, as this last decade of the nineteenth century was to see an unprecedented rise in interest in coastal excursions throughout the British Isles. Indeed, these were the halcyon days, *Princess Alice* or not.

***The Shah*, later renamed *Penelope*, was one of four river steamers built in 1889 for the River Thames Steamboat Company that were later passed to the Victoria Steamboat Association.**

The Victoria Steamboat Association was, of course, not alone on the Thames, with the GSN fleet maintaining the lead on the London to Thanet ports, and the Medway Steam Packet Company operating the cross-river ferry and excursions from Medway ports to Southend. The latter town received a fillip in 1889 when the new iron pier, 'the world's longest pleasure pier', was completed. The pier was lengthened for the 1898 season, providing additional berths for the steamers.

With the retrenching of the former River Thames Steamboat Company in 1886, two related developments took place in quick succession. One was an initiative by a business syndicate in Clacton-on-Sea, which wanted to introduce a new company to try and recover the steamer trade to the town. The other was a spate of new orders by GSN in response to rumours that the new operator from Clacton would be equipped with modern, fast and luxurious ships, and which now, in any event, saw an opportunity to enter the Essex coast trade. GSN was also conscious of increasing competition on its traditional Thanet and cross-Channel services and was seeking new trade – what better than a service to Southend and on to Clacton-on-Sea and Great Yarmouth?

One year the town of Clacton was totally isolated from its daily patronage from the London steamer, the next it was swamped. It had taken only a few weeks for the syndicate of local traders and businessmen to launch its own company to be known as The London, Woolwich & Clacton-on-Sea Steamboat Company. Mr Horace Spence was put in charge as Manager, and the company's registered office was opened at 33 Walbrook in London EC. In addition, an order was placed with J. Scott of Kinghorn in Fife for a smart little steamer with compound machinery.

The new steamer was given the obvious name of *Clacton* and was ready for the 1888 season. Based at Old Swan Pier, she commenced her daily routine of London to Clacton and back. The *Clacton* was hugely successful, although a bit small for the run at only 241 tons gross. At the end of the season the company directors decided to issue a 5% dividend to the shareholders, who were of course themselves, and to sell the *Clacton*, while planning an order for a larger and faster vessel for the 1889 season.

In my history of GSN (*Birds of the Sea: 150 Years of the General Steam Navigation Company*) I wrote:

> 'GSN embarked on its new building programme with orders for five new saloon steamers also placed with J. Scott in Fife. These were the famous "classical bird" class of steamers, the first of which, the *Halcyon*, was delivered in 1887 and the last, the *Philomel*, at a cost of £13,230 in 1889. The other three ships were given the names *Mavis*, *Oriole* and *Laverock*, the latter built at a cost of £12,150. They were all of broadly similar dimensions, although the *Oriole* and *Philomel* were 20 feet or so longer than their sisters and had more powerful engines, the *Philomel* significantly so, with a nominal horsepower of 327 compared with 240 to 260 in the other vessels. The engines were of the compound, two-crank, diagonal type, lubricated by grease delivered by 'walking tubes', as used on some naval ships of the day. Their service speed was a comfortable 17 knots.
>
> The five "classical birds" offered saloon accommodation forward of the single funnel, the rounded fore end of the saloon ending just behind the foremast. Their distinguishing features were the full-width saloon and the Upper Deck carried forward to the foremast. They all had two masts.
>
> In recognition of their role as pleasure steamers, they were given cream-coloured funnels and white deckhouses instead of the more utilitarian darker colours that were then standard. The ships took over the Thanet and continental trips from London Bridge, and inaugurated a two-day return to Great Yarmouth, with intermediate calls including Gravesend, Southend and Clacton. The *Laverock* was also used in 1889 for excursions to Boulogne, the popularity of which was boosted by visitors to the Paris Exhibition. The older ships *Sir Walter Raleigh* and *Hoboken* ... were retained, largely for relief work, but the new quintet sent the *Eagle* to the breakers in 1886, with the now outdated *Hilda* following three years later.'

The halcyon days had indeed begun, although the *Halcyon* managed to collide with, and sink, the tug

Above left **The *Halcyon* (1887) was the first of a quintet of steamers delivered by J. Scott at Kinghorn.**

Left **The *Oriole* (1888), with a full complement of passengers aboard.**

Below left **The *Laverock* (1889), another of GSN's 'classical bird' quintet, seen at sea complete with staysail.**

Above **The *Philomel* (1889) was distinctive in having two large ventilators forward on the Boat Deck.**

Sunbeam off Wapping in 1889, happily without loss of life!

Meanwhile, the London, Woolwich & Clacton-on-Sea Steamboat Company was unable to take delivery of its new ship, the replacement for the *Clacton*, until May 1890. The Victoria Steamboat Association obliged by putting a ship on the Clacton run in 1889 to maintain the business momentum.

Delays in building the new vessel for the Clacton syndicate were incurred through difficulties in raising the necessary finance. In the end, an order was placed on 27 June 1889 with William Denny & Company of Dumbarton. The contract price was £19,000, to be paid in four instalments of £3,000 while building, and the balance to be paid off in annual instalments of £1,000 with interest due at 5%. The new ship, the *Clacton Belle*, inaugurated the famous 'Belle' nomenclature, ultimately allowing the cumbersome name of the owning company, the London, Woolwich & Clacton Steamboat Company to be reduced to just Belle Steamers Limited in 1897. The *Clacton Belle* was a much more substantial ship than the *Clacton*, with a gross tonnage of 458 and a speed of 17 knots derived from compound diagonal engines. She ran her first season in tandem with a vessel from the Victoria Steamboat Company.

A distinctive feature of the ship was her telescopic funnel, which had an ominous tilt to starboard. A fixed funnel with a cowl top replaced this in 1900 when the London base moved to Fresh Wharf, below London Bridge. In her early days the *Clacton Belle* carried stay sails for use with a fair wind and to inhibit excessive rolling. She was also equipped with traditional wooden paddle floats, which tended to work free, causing significant delays and consequent annoyance to passengers while they were reinstalled. She was a two-class ship, with the saloon slightly better appointed than the fore cabin. Caterers were

The *Clacton Belle* (1890) as built, with a telescopic funnel and before the forward saloon was built nearly to the foremast, probably in the winter of 1893/94.

contracted to the ship and described in a contemporary guide as 'distinctly good'.

The owners were so pleased with the *Clacton Belle* that all subsequent new orders also went to Denny (see Table 3). The next ship, delivered in 1891, was also the smallest, specifically designed, as written in her builder's contract, for trading between Ipswich and Clacton. This was the *Woolwich Belle*, and she was equipped with compound engines that gave her a speed of 15 knots, essentially a smaller and slower version of the *Clacton Belle*. However, the first two years of her career were spent on the London to Clacton route, displacing the Victoria Steamboat Association steamer and running alongside the *Clacton Belle*. The *Woolwich Belle* had a telescopic funnel to allow passage beneath London Bridge, but unlike her larger sister did not have a bow rudder for the long stern-first haul up to Fresh Wharf, although this was added later on in her career.

A feeder service was available from Clacton to Ipswich by the Victoria Steamboat Association's *Fairy Queen*, formerly the *Queen of the Orwell*, under River Thames Steamboat Company management, and through tickets could be obtained from London. However, in 1893 this service was taken over by the Clacton company, when the *Woolwich Belle* was transferred from the London service to provide Clacton and Walton services to Harwich, Felixstowe and Ipswich, where a special pontoon provided her overnight berth. The Great Eastern Railway also maintained

The *Woolwich Belle* (1891) in the River Orwell, as built. A forward saloon was added in 1912.

Table 3: Belle Steamers fleet list

Name	Built	Tons gross	Length (ft)	Speed (knots)	Comments
Clacton[1]	1888	241	190	~13	Sold 1889 to H. Surgonje, Turkey, renamed *Aidin*, out of register 1913
Clacton Belle[1]	1890	458	246	17	Scrapped at Grays 1929
Woolwich Belle[1]	1891	298	200	15	Renamed *Queen of the South* 1922. Scrapped at Grays 1932
London Belle[1]	1893	738	280	19	Scrapped at Grays 1929
Southend Belle[1]	1896	570	249	18	Renamed *Laguna Belle* 1929. Scrapped at Nieuw Lekkerkerk 1946
Walton Belle[2]	1897	465	230	17	Renamed *Essex Queen* 1926 and *Pride of Devon* 1946. Scrapped at Grays 1951
Yarmouth Belle[3]	1898	522	240	17	Renamed *Queen of Southend* 1928 and *Thames Queen* 1938. Scrapped on the Tyne 1947
Southwold Belle[3]	1900	535	245	17	Renamed *Westernland* 1912 and *Bon Voyage* 1913. Scrapped at Genoa 1925

[1] Built for London, Woolwich & Clacton-on-Sea Steamboat Company
[2] Built for Belle Steamers
[3] Built for Coast Development Company

up to six round-trip sailings a day from Ipswich to Harwich and Felixstowe using the paddlers *Orwell*, *Stour* and *Norfolk* until 1895, when the new double-ended steamers *Suffolk* and *Essex* were introduced and later joined by a new *Norfolk*. The railway service continued until 1931, although the *Essex* was sold to Henry Cooney of Westcliffe-on-Sea and briefly used as an excursion steamer at Southend in 1914, before she moved to Humber ferry duties during the Great War.

The *Woolwich Belle* was displaced from the premier London East Coast service in 1893 by the arrival of the largest member of the fleet, the *London Belle*. This new vessel was designed to face the head-on competition from the Victoria Steamboat Association and its prestigious sisters *Koh-I-Noor* and *Royal Sovereign*, which arrived in the Thames in 1892 and 1893 respectively. The *Koh-I-Noor* had already eroded traffic on the East Coast service and the *London Belle* was the response. However, before she could enter service a 1,200-foot-long extension to Clacton Pier had to be designed and completed. The contract with Denny stated that the ship was 'to beat the rival *Koh-I-Noor* (building by Fairfield) and to have a BoT Certificate No 2 for Channel service'. In the event, the *London Belle* was commissioned in May 1893, one year after her rival the *Koh-I-Noor*.

The Denny-built *London Belle* was innovative, being the first Thames paddler to have triple-expansion engines, a system all subsequent 'Belle' steamers were to adopt. Indeed, she was the first triple-expansion-engined paddle steamer to be built by William Denny, although that firm had previously installed triple-expansion engines in screw steamers. Her speed of 19 knots equalled anything on the river, although she was 30 feet shorter in length than the *Koh-I-Noor*. The Promenade Deck ran from the foremast almost to the stern, providing a most imposing appearance. Although the *London Belle* was built with a fixed funnel, the foremast was hinged to allow her to berth at Fresh Wharf with the prow of the ship beneath London Bridge. For the next three years the *London Belle* and *Clacton Belle* maintained the London to Clacton service, and the *Woolwich Belle* provided the feeder service and excursions at Clacton.

The Great Eastern Railway steamer *Essex* (1895) on the River Orwell leaving Ipswich.

Sister ship *Suffolk* (1895) alongside the Halfpenny Pier at Harwich.

The Victoria Steamboat Association (VSA), as the successor to the River Thames Steamboat Company, was about to fall on its feet. At the end of its first season VSA bought the famous Clyde steamer *Lord of the Isles* from the Glasgow & Inveraray Steamboat Company and placed her on service on the Thames in the spring of 1891. She had been built in 1877 at Partick, by D. & W. Henderson & Company, and was one of the first steamers to be fitted with low-voltage direct-current electric light. *The Lord of the Isles* caused a sensation, being large, fast and comfortable. The fore and aft saloons were not full-width, as on the 'Belle' steamers, but had alleyways either side. The aft saloon was widened after her first season on the Thames to full width, but this alteration seriously detracted from her appearance. So impressed were the Directors of VSA with the Inverary company's funnel colours that they remained unchanged and thereafter were adopted by VSA – a red and black top with two white bands and a central white band near the top of the red section.

VSA had inherited a variety of up-river and below-bridge vessels, the latter including the *Duke of Cambridge*, *Duke of Edinburgh*, *Glen Rosa* and *Queen of the Orwell* (which it had renamed *Fairy Queen*). It also had the former Thames Steamboat Company's London Bridge to Greenwich steamers, *Azalea*, *Ceres*, *Lily*, *Osprey*, *Princess Mary*, *Prince of Wales*, *Primrose*, *Rose*, *Rifleman*, *Shamrock*, *Thistle* and *Vesta*, the *Ceres* taking the pensioners prize, having been built in 1844. These little ships passed to the Thames Steamboat Company (1897) Limited, for which three new river steamers were commissioned in 1898, the *Alexandra*, *Bodicea* and *Cleopatra*.

But none could vie with the *Lord of the Isles*, a comparatively massive iron-hulled steamer. She

Right The *London Belle* (1893) was specifically designed to compete with the *Koh-I-Noor*.

Below The *Koh-I-Noor* (1892) suffering 'soldier's wind' in the Thames.

Right The *Royal Sovereign* (1893) in New Palace Steamers colours and showing her telescopic funnels.

The *Lord of the Isles* (1877) retained the colours of her former owner, the Glasgow & Inveraray Steamboat Company, when she was acquired by the Victoria Steamboat Association in 1891.

was propelled by diagonal oscillating engines, with a massive stroke of 66 inches in a 46-inch-diameter cylinder, a system popular for steamers on the longer Clyde routes in the 1860s and 1870s. Her twin 'haystack' boilers necessitated two funnels set well apart. The *Lord of the Isles* worked alongside the *Glen Rosa*, and each was equipped with telescopic funnels to get to their London berth, which was still at the Old Swan Pier above London Bridge.

Armed with the obvious success of the *Lord of the Isles*, VSA suddenly found itself being canvassed by the Govan-based Fairfield Shipbuilding & Engineering Company to manage two brand-new crack steamers, to be paid for on long-term instalments. Fairfield had edged its way into the fast steamer market, placing the *Queen Victoria* and *Prince of Wales* on the Liverpool to Douglas route in 1887 to create a price war with the established operator, the Isle of Man Steam Packet Company. As originally intended by Fairfield, the Steam Packet Company then bought the two steamers the following year.

The hire-purchase arrangement offered to VSA reflected the earlier arrangement between Fairfield and the newly formed Liverpool & North Wales Steamship Company, which had received the heavily mortgaged new steamer *St Tudno* in 1891. The new steamers destined for the Thames were each developments of the *St Tudno*, respectively the *Koh-I-Noor*, delivered to VSA in 1892, and the *Royal Sovereign*, delivered to a financially separate company, the London & East Coast Express Steamship Service, in 1893, but managed by VSA. In addition, the magnificent steamer *La Marguerite* followed in 1894 under another holding company, Palace Steamers. Together, these ships made the GSN fleet look very plainly furnished and second-rate.

Each ship was effectively mortgaged from the shipbuilder. The *Koh-I-Noor*, for example, had been built at a cost of £50,900. This was a lot of money in those far-off days, and contrasts with the contract price of £35,360 for her rival, the *London Belle*, reflecting the sumptuous décor and style of completion adopted for the Fairfield/VSA ship. Despite being a huge success as a trend-setter on the Thames, VSA found it was unable to keep up the payments on the vessels, and Fairfield foreclosed the mortgages in 1894. Fairfield then established a new operating company for the fleet under the name New Palace Steamers.

Nothing quite like this trio had ever graced the Thames before. The Thames steamers had always lagged behind their Clyde counterparts; for example, the early saloon steamers such as MacBrayne's three steamers named *Iona* and its *Columba* were never replicated on the Thames. Indeed the second-hand *Lord of the Isles* had made a tremendous impact with excursionists when she retired from the Clyde to pick up service on the Thames at the age of 13. But what of the three new ships themselves? The first two, the *Koh-I-Noor* and *Royal Sovereign*, were near sisters, although different in appearance, as the latter had the engine and boiler rooms placed some 12 feet forward of those of her sister, providing a more balanced profile of funnels and foremast.

The two ships were not only big, at 884 and 892 tons gross respectively, but were also technically very advanced. Built entirely of steel, they were subdivided into water-tight compartments, so that the first class dining saloon had to be divided into two parts, one on either side of the dividing bulkhead. They had the modern two-cylinder diagonal engine configuration and the paddle floats were of the contemporary curved design. With engines providing 3,500 indicated horsepower, the pair were fit for 19 knots. They had bow rudders set into the stem to facilitate steerage while going astern, a particularly useful feature whenever leaving Old Swan Pier above London Bridge.

One nice touch was the emblems decorating the paddle boxes. The *Koh-I-Noor* had a representation of the famous diamond given to Queen Victoria in 1850 at the annexation of Punjab, while the *Royal Sovereign* portrayed the monarch's head.

The two deck saloons, fore and aft of the machinery spaces, provided a continuous Promenade Deck from the bows, with an open deck space below, forward of the deck saloon, and extending almost to the stern. This design had been pioneered on the Clyde by the Caledonian Steam Packet Company's *Duchess of Hamilton*, which had been commissioned in 1890. It meant that the fore and aft rope handlers could neither be seen from, nor could they see, the bridge on the *Koh-I-Noor* or the *Royal Sovereign*, and the consequent communication difficulty occasionally created problems at some piers. The ships each sported a bookstall, a fruit stall, hairdresser and barber, and a Post Office (at last catching up with the standards set by the MacBrayne steamers), and had low-voltage direct-current electric lighting throughout.

An unfortunate delivery voyage from the Clyde required the *Koh-I-Noor* to return to her builders to have a new bow section installed, following a stranding off the Pembrokeshire coast. Six weeks later she finally arrived on station and commenced on the Old Swan Pier to Southend and Clacton service, displacing *Glen Rosa*, which was initially chartered to a South Coast operator and later bought by P. & A. Campbell. Once left with no steamers, Clacton now had its own Belle Steamers, as well as GSN and VSA competing for patronage. Delivery of the *Royal Sovereign* was more straightforward. She displaced the *Koh-I-Noor* from the Essex route, allowing the *Koh-I-Noor* to go head-to-head with the GSN 'classical bird' steamers on the Thanet services.

Competition was hotting up, but the best was yet to come. This was the *La Marguerite*, built specifically for the Tilbury to Boulogne day excursion service via Margate, and named after a daughter of Arnold Williams, one of the founders of VSA. With a gross tonnage of 1,554, *La Marguerite* was too large and fast to be usefully deployed further upstream than Tilbury, and in any case special train connections were run to bring the Londoners down from Fenchurch Street to the departure point. As good as anything the London, Chatham & Dover Railway had at Dover, the new 20-knot 'cross-Channel excursion' steamer was a huge success.

Described as a swagger ship, she was hugely popular, being both large and with accommodation of a very high standard. A contemporary guide to London described the ship as follows:

> 'Those who are accustomed to steamboat excursions from London need no introduction to *La Marguerite*, which the Fairfield company built for the owners of the New Palace Steamers. When she was launched, in the early summer of 1894, it was claimed that she was the largest vessel afloat adventuring on daily voyages. *La Marguerite* is licensed to carry 3,000 passengers as far as Margate, and 2,000 across the Channel. She is 330 feet long, 40 feet broad (73 feet across the paddles) and 26 feet deep. Her hull is of steel, and she is lighted throughout by electricity, while the luxurious fittings on board do not belie the description of her as a "floating palace".'

La Marguerite: the swagger ship

In his book *Steamers of North Wales*, F. C. Thornley wrote fondly of *La Marguerite*, which, of course, ended her days on the Liverpool and North Wales excursion circuit:

> 'The vessel was divided into 11 watertight compartments. Her engines were of the two-cylinder compound diagonal type having a nominal horse power of 857, the high-pressure cylinder was of 56 inches and the low-pressure 110 inches, the stroke of the pistons being 72 inches.
>
> The accommodation on *La Marguerite* was spacious and comfortable, that of the saloon passengers was situated aft, as was the custom of that period, the second class being in the fore part of the ship. The whole of the extensive Promenade Deck was reserved for the saloon passengers. On it and situated between the funnels, was the bridge and also the ship's shop for the sale of chocolates, books and souvenirs. On the Upper Deck was situated a large and comfortable saloon, where light refreshments were available, and also on this deck were the Purser's office and private cabins. The after part of the Main Deck was occupied by the main dining saloon, which extended the full width of the ship, and further forward on this deck one could view the engine room through a series of windows. The engines always attracted attention, and whenever one passed that way one was always sure to see a considerable "gallery" watching the massive engines in motion. On the Lower Deck was a large and handsomely panelled smoke room. The second class accommodation was equally good of its kind.
>
> ...*La Marguerite* took her first sailing to France on 23 June 1894, and her arrival at Boulogne was greeted with much enthusiasm, thousands cheering her as she entered the harbour. Bands played "God Save the Queen" and this was responded to by musicians aboard *La Marguerite* who played "La Marseillaise". The Mayor, Corporation, and Chamber of Commerce of Boulogne were entertained on board, speeches were made, toasts drunk, and there was a general air of festivity.'

Thornley recounts several other anecdotes including:

> 'One summer evening in the nineties great consternation was caused in London and on the Thames-side by a rumour that *La Marguerite* had gone down in the Channel with great loss of life. The rumour became so persistent that it was published in the evening papers and, with the *Princess Alice* disaster of 1878 still fresh in the minds of the London public, one can imagine the anxiety which it caused. Later when it was proved to be untrue and the excitement had died down, the origin of it was discovered.'

Someone had misinterpreted the Harbour Master saying, '*La Marguerite* has gone down,' missing out the vital two words 'the river'!

What Thornley neglects to report is that, as the passengers spent a total of 9 hours at sea during the day trip, many of them were in high spirits by the time Boulogne was reached, and many more were incapable of even standing by the time they were returned to Tilbury in the evening. The husband's 'I am just going down to see the engines' was, for many, a neat excuse to meet with friends in the bar!

Even the mighty *La Marguerite* had one design fault. Captain J. H. Isherwood reported in *Sea Breezes* in May 1983:

> 'Some of the piers she was to use were low, so her sponsons had to be low also so that the piers should not get below them (with disastrous results). This resulted, in rough weather, in the sponsons thudding down on waves at times and causing the

lavatories on the sponsons themselves to be suddenly flooded (with more disastrous results!).'

On cross-Channel days, passengers left Fenchurch Street for Tilbury at 7.10 or 8.30am on special boat trains, and were back in the city about 9.15 that evening. This gave continental travellers an hour ashore, and Margate visitors about 6 hours, but with an optional sea cruise as an alternative. On Margate-only days, the schedule was a bit more relaxed, with departure from 9.45am and return to Fenchurch Street at 6.30 in the evening.

In spite of her great popularity, the ship was expensive to run and maintain, and the seasons were short. New Palace Steamers eventually found that she was not recovering the payments needed on her mortgage to her builders, and Fairfield in turn decided to deploy the ship elsewhere. Transferred in 1904 to the Liverpool & North Wales Steamship Company, lower wages, cheaper coal and slower operating speeds brought the big ship back into profit. Captain J. Young was appointed to the vessel and it was he who later took her to war as a cross-Channel troop ship. After a short period on charter to the Isle of Man Steam Packet Company, *La Marguerite* returned to the North Wales excursion service in May 1920, but her age was now against her and she was an increasingly expensive unit to maintain. Withdrawn and scrapped in 1925, the ship's bell was presented to the 1st Battalion of the 6th Regiment of the City of London Rifles, the first battalion *La Marguerite* had taken across to France in the war. The bell now forms part of the City of London Rifles' memorial in the Church of the Holy Sepulchre in central London.

The *La Marguerite* quickly earned a regular following on her daily run. She was allowed Friday off for maintenance, for the most part lying in the river below Gravesend, but was found to be a very reliable and economical unit. This was the first example of economy of scale in the Thames excursion fleet; she was also ultimately the largest excursion paddle steamer ever to be built.

The *La Marguerite* was not, however, the pioneer of day return trips from the Thames to Boulogne. These were inaugurated in the 1870s by the small paddle tug *Undaunted*, under the command of Captain Jack Spicer, the owner's son. Whenever he passed between the piers on arrival at Boulogne he would amuse passengers and onlookers alike by climbing onto one of the paddle boxes to play 'La Marseillaise' on his violin! This musical eccentricity was also pioneering, as the excursion ship's bands perpetuated the playing of 'La Marseillaise' on arrival at Boulogne well into the 1930s.

Despite competition between the three key players, business was maintained by an expanding demand from Londoners wishing to flee their grimy city for a day excursion to the coast or the continent. A couple of new-start companies had in the meantime come and gone. The *Bonnie Doon* ran in the late summer of 1887 to Clacton from Fresh Wharf, out one day, returning the next, on charter to Richard Ford. This followed the withdrawal of the River Thames Steamboat Company, but, despite a monopoly at that time, she failed within weeks. Burtt described the mess:

> 'In a police court case Richard Ford, ship charterer, answered several summonses. Samuel Middleton stated that he had been engaged by the defendant to meet the *Bonnie Doon*, swing her and moor her. He also had to do other work connected with the ship and his wage amounted to £1 16s 0d. Captain Mason [formerly master of the *Glen Rosa*] stated that he was engaged by the defendant from 29 July to 15 October at a wage of £7 per week. The defendant owed him three weeks' wages. Joseph Haw said he was engaged as Chief Steward at £2 per week, and when the ship stopped he was to receive £10 gratuity. The ship had stopped running because the merchants refused to supply her with coal as the coal bill was not paid. The Magistrate made orders for the various amounts claimed to be paid.'

The *Bonnie Doon* (1876) seen in the final chapter of her life working for P. & A. Campbell at Eastbourne.

Slightly more successful was another Clyde steamer, the *Arran*, which entered the Thames excursion trade in 1888. Captain Mason was also in command of this little steamer for parts of the 1890 and 1891 seasons, after which she was sold for use as a tug in Ireland. Her roster was Fresh Wharf to Southend and on to Sheerness. In doing so, she provided a wake-up call to the Medway Steam Packet Company, which in 1888 responded by buying the five-year-old iron-hulled steamer *Lady Margaret* from her Cardiff owners, the Bristol Channel Express Steamboat Company, for which she had failed to pay her way on the Cardiff to Weston ferry. Although only 144 tons gross, she was bigger than her elderly wooden-hulled fleet-mates, the *City of Rochester* dating from 1847, the *Alma* and *Lady of Lorne*. The acquisition of the *Lady Margaret* placed the Medway Steam Packet Company on a more solid foundation and it may be that the threat posed by the arrival of the *Arran* actually saved the company from oblivion.

The *Lady Margaret* served her new owners well, receiving a new funnel in 1902 at the company's own shipyard, the Acorn yard at Rochester. Sadly, the ship caught fire alongside the Acorn Wharf the following year, and while all useful fittings were removed, she ended her days at the scrapyard. This left the company rather exposed, as the old *City of Rochester* had been scrapped in 1897, and the *Lady of Lorne* had been sold two years later, leaving only the elderly *Alma* alone to maintain the Sheerness, Chatham and Rochester service.

5. THE LAST VICTORIANS

New Palace Steamers, which was almost wholly owned by Fairfield Shipbuilding & Engineering of Govan, had taken over the Victoria Steamboat Association's down-river services at the end of the 1894 season. Its three crack steamers took up service the following year with plain yellow funnels. The *Royal Sovereign* remained on the Southend and Margate station, the *Koh-I-Noor* on the Clacton route and the magnificent *La Marguerite* served between Tilbury and Boulogne. New Palace Steamers also inherited the *Glen Rosa*, which, until 1895, had been used on a feeder service from Great Yarmouth to Harwich, where she connected with the *Koh-I-Noor* on the alternate days that the London steamer terminated at Harwich rather than Clacton. For the next two years, however, the *Glen Rosa* was placed in direct opposition to the Medway Steam Packet Company on its Southend to Sheerness and Rochester route. With the introduction of new tonnage by the Medway Steam Packet Company, the *Glen Rosa* was sold at the end of the 1896 season to P. & A. Campbell for use on the South Coast.

The *Lord of the Isles* was also still much in demand, providing relief services on the down-river routes and providing additional services at peak times. However, she was now quite dated and was becoming mechanically unreliable, even demolishing her two funnels under London Bridge due to engine failure. L. G. Lane, commenting in 1934 on the incident, observed wryly: 'Approaching, she had seen Palace Steamers go under the bridge with impunity and thought she could do the same.'

The *Lord of the Isles* was sold in 1896 to Mrs C. P. Black, and placed under the management of Mr Peter Blair Black, an associate of the Victoria Steamboat Association. Separate ownership and management was almost certainly a device to protect the vessel should the fledgling company be forced into bankruptcy, a wise precaution as will be seen. The *Lord of the Isles* started to ply her one-ship London to Southend and Margate roster and was in due course renamed *Jupiter*, and marketed under the banner Planet Steamers.

The *Lord of the Isles* was replaced in the New Palace Steamers fleet by another former Clyde excursion steamer, the *Victoria*. She was a handsome two-funnelled vessel that had originally been part of the Wemyss Bay Steamship Company's fleet of Campbell & Gillies. In April 1890 Campbell & Gillies unilaterally withdrew from the rail and sea partnership it had been enjoying with the Caledonian Railway and its associated steamer fleet on the Glasgow, Wemyss Bay and Rothesay services, and put the displaced ships up for sale. Consequently, the *Victoria* was operated as an excursion steamer firstly on Belfast Lough, then back on the Clyde for much of the next five years before she was bought by the London & East Coast Express Steamship Company (former owners of the *Royal Sovereign*).

The *Victoria* was placed under the management of New Palace Steamers, and was marketed under her owner's name in competition with the *Royal Sovereign*. This was an early example of branding in order to develop the market, a tactic that is represented today by Carnival Cruises, with their diverse competing brands such as P&O Cruises, Princess Cruises and Cunard. It also reflects the common practice of Victorian ship-owners to hold shares in competing companies.

The *Victoria* remained on the Southend and Clacton service for only two seasons before she returned to the Clyde in 1897. There she was put to work during 1903 under the title 'Victorian Pleasure Cruising', ending her days working alongside the *Lady of the Isles*, which was none other than the former *Jupiter*, ex-*Lord of the Isles*.

Winter tugs and summer excursion steamers

While the prestige ships of New Palace Steamers represented one end of the spectrum, a number of tugs was still employed throughout the 1890s and beyond, offering seasonal excursions at niche locations. In fact, the practice continued even after the Great War in some places; for example, the United Towing Company's Hull-based tug *Yorkshireman* retired from summer cruising at Bridlington only in 1955. Further up the East Coast, the famous Scarborough-based paddle excursion steamer *Bilsdale* had pleased the holidaymakers there between 1924 and 1934, but had started life in 1900 as the *Lord Roberts* for the Great Yarmouth

Left **The Great Yarmouth Steam Tug Company's wooden-hulled steamer *United Service* (1871) operated seasonal excursions until the 1930s.**

Below **The *Lord Nelson* (1896) seen leaving Yarmouth some time in the 1900s.**

Steam Tug Company. At Yarmouth she and the 1896-built *Lord Nelson*, in company with the elderly passenger tug *United Service*, dating from 1871, provided 2-or-3-hour cruises out to the St Nicholas Lightship, Scroby Sands and the Belle Buoy, and along the coast towards Cromer or Lowestoft. The *Lord Roberts* was sold in 1910, although the excursions continued, the *United Service* only being scrapped in 1942.

Another popular tug in the 1890s was the *Conquerer*, owned by William Sandford of Gravesend and under the command of Captain Robert Andrews. She spent the summers running excursions between Margate and Folkestone before being sold to the Admiralty in 1896. She was followed by a new twin-funnelled ship of the same name built in 1897, which continued the tradition of summer cruises from the Thanet ports, sometimes as far afield as Southend and Calais. She was later transferred to Southend for a short period and in the early 1900s offered a direct service between London and Dover, a route later adopted by GSN. This service had been pioneered in 1867 by the one-year-old steamer *Albert Victor*, owned by the Saloon Steam Packet Company – outwards one day and return the next, although her route was terminated at Margate in subsequent years with a connecting steamer going on to Dover.

On the death of William Sandford in 1903 the *Conquerer* was sold to Dick & Page. She retained her grey hull with white upperworks, but lost the white stars on her yellow funnels. Thereafter, during the winter months she was used for 'seeking and salvage', for which duties she was known as the 'Grey Ghost'. Again based in the summer at Margate from 1909 to 1914 she took over the popular Margate, Deal, Dover to Folkestone run from the railway steamers *Myleta* and *Edward William*, which were then disposed of. The *Conquerer* was advertised at that time to feature a band. Eric Harrison, in a letter to *Sea Breezes* in April 1968, reports:

> 'The so-called band turned out to be one violin accompanied by a harmonium, and after scraping and treading through two or three numbers "half the band" would immediately go round with a collecting box.'

He continues:

> 'The service was run by Dick & Page themselves; both the Folkestone Council and the Chamber of Trade had actively negotiated in 1909 to arrange a coastal service after the South Eastern & Chatham Railway finished theirs. P. & A. Campbell was approached but regretted it had no steamer available, though it did arrange for one of the Brighton-based ships to make a number of trips to Folkestone in those years.'

The *Conquerer* was sold to the Jersey Steam Shipping Company in 1920 and later briefly used for excursion work on the Forth, where she now offered a real live band and dancing, a ladies' saloon and a bar. She was scrapped in 1925 after ending her career as the *Hurworth*, and later the *Hutton Cross* for the Tees Towing Company. It was reported by an employee of Ship Towage (London) Limited in the 1960s that one of his father's first jobs was collecting the fares on the *Conquerer* when she was running between Margate and Southend. Apparently he was always horribly seasick and disliked the work intensely!

The well-known towage firm of William Watkins was also engaged in seasonal excursion services. The company deployed the twin-funnelled sea-going paddle tug *India*, dating from 1876, at Margate for the summers of 1890 to 1893. The *India* was built of iron and had two side-lever engines and surface condenser-type boilers. Her master, George Harris, received a wage of 35 shillings per week plus a percentage of the tug's earnings by way of an incentive. The vessel carried a mainsail that conserved coal while seeking homeward-bound sailing ships in the winter months.

F. Bracey Cook, in a letter to *Sea Breezes* in November 1950, recalled the *India* and the many passenger yachts that worked from the jetties at Ramsgate and Margate:

'I wonder if there are any who can recall the [passenger] yachts that used to work from Margate Jetty. One was the *Moss Rose* and I think the other was called *Sunbeam*. I remember that if the slant of the wind was right, the yachts and Watkins's tug *India* would do the trip out to the Tongue Lightship and back, and the yachts would be first home.'

The *India* was sold in January 1894 to J. Constant for £1,000. She went on charter work on the South Coast where duties included excursions and occasional trips to Cherbourg catering for 300 passengers. She was replaced by the brand-new steamer *Cynthia*, which was especially built for excursion work. However, the *Cynthia* was redeployed to the Tyne from 1896, as competition increased in the Thames in the early 1900s. In 1905 she was under the ownership of the Hastings, St Leonards & Eastbourne Steamboat Company before she was again sold, this time for use in Ireland. At one point she offered 'Tea Dansant Cruises' from Bangor, Co Down – afternoon tea, dancing and a sea trip for 2s 6d. She was wrecked in a storm in 1933 when she broke free from her moorings inside Dun Laoghaire Harbour.

In 1892 the Margate Steam Yacht Company bought the side-lever-engined paddle tug *Cambria*. She had been built by T. Redhead & Company in 1879, which also operated her as a tug until 1890 before she took up work as an excursion steamer, initially for the Southport Steamship Company. In 1893 the *Cambria* passed into the ownership of Dausey & Robinson, still registered at Ramsgate, and still employed on short-duration local cruises out of Margate. This second season at Margate was her last and she was then sold to French owners, later ending her days at Scarborough and elsewhere in the North of England. Her name remained unchanged throughout her career; she was scrapped in 1935.

Table 4: Steamers of the Victoria Steamboat Association (VSA), 1890-95 (down-river vessels only) and those operated by New Palace Steamers (and associate companies), 1895-1918

Name	Built	Tons gross	Length (ft)	Speed (knots)	Comments
Duke of Cambridge	1866	92	151		Ex-*Ardgowan* (1875), scrapped 1898 as owned by VSA
Duke of Edinburgh	1870	123	175		Ex-*Craigrownie* (1875), scrapped 1898 as owned by VSA
Queen of the Orwell	1862	172	165		Renamed *Fairy Queen* 1891, to VSA 1897
Glen Rosa	1877	296	206	20	First came to Thames in 1881; sold for service on South Coast 1896
Lord of the Isles	1877	451	246	19	Bought 1890, renamed *Jupiter* 1896 for Planet Steamers
Victoria	1886	341	224		Bought 1895, sold 1900
Koh-I-Noor	1892	884	300	19	Sold for scrap after lay-up throughout First World War
Royal Sovereign	1893	891	300	19	Sold to Royal Sovereign Steamship Company 1918 (laid up throughout First World War)
La Marguerite	1894	1,554	350	21	Transferred to Liverpool after 1903 season
La Belgique	1875	484	220	14	1897 season only

Apparently, about this time there were some marvellous scenes of passengers storming ashore over closed pier gates at Dunoon and breaking the quiet of the Sabbath, much to the amazement of Dunoon residents.

The new steamer introduced by the Medway Steam Packet Company, to see off the intruding Palace Steamers' *Glen Rosa*, was the *Princess of Wales*. She was a fine modern paddler built at Middlesbrough by R. Craggs & Sons and delivered to the company in 1896. She was of modest proportions, being some 163 tons gross with compound diagonal engines, supplying a mere 65 nominal horsepower. Nevertheless, she was enough to send New Palace Steamers scurrying. The *Princess of Wales* ran alongside the *Lady Margaret* (see Chapter 3) and her arrival allowed the retirement of the elderly wooden steamers, *City of Rochester*, *Alma* and *Lady of Lorne*, the latter pair being retained in reserve for a further two years before being sold for scrap.

The Clacton Belle fleet of steamers was also expanded with the delivery of a further four 'Belles', commissioned over the four years 1896 to 1900. Having already used the three place names for its ships that made up the full company title (The London, Woolwich & Clacton-on-sea Steamboat Company), the newcomers were given the names *Southend Belle*, *Walton Belle*, *Yarmouth Belle* and *Southwold Belle* (see Table 3, page 41).

The *Princess of Wales* (1896) passing Frindsbury on the Medway.

The arrival of the *Walton Belle* in 1897 enabled the company to take on both GSN and New Palace Steamers on the lucrative London to Herne Bay, Margate and Ramsgate route, together with a regular weekly service to Clacton, Walton and Great Yarmouth. The *Yarmouth Belle* was designed principally for the express East Coast service between London and Yarmouth. Once the final ship of the fleet, the *Southwold Belle*, was in place in 1900, the company ran a variety of additional routes including London to Southend and round the Nore Light, and occasional services between Clacton to Margate.

The design speed for the *Southwold Belle* was 17½ knots, half a knot greater than that of her sisters. It was customary in the days of steam for the builders to employ two sets of crews, one to man ships on trials and one to man them before the ships were actually delivered to the owners. There were the elite crews, whose job it was to work the vessel up to its absolute peak performance during the owner's acceptance trials, while the delivery crew would take the ship wherever it was to be deployed. The stokers and firemen in the elite crews were second to none, and if they could not get the ship up to the contract speed over the measured mile no

Left The *Southend Belle* (1896) packed with passengers and with steam discharging from the forward rope-handling gear.

Left The *Walton Belle* (1897) at Yarmouth.

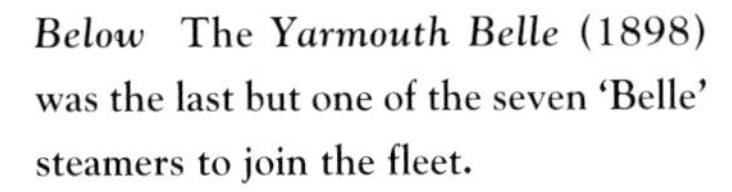

Below The *Yarmouth Belle* (1898) was the last but one of the seven 'Belle' steamers to join the fleet.

The *Southwold Belle* (1900) on a morning departure from Fresh Wharf.

subsequent crew would ever approach it. Sadly the elite crew did not receive their performance bonus with the *Southwold Belle* as she only ever managed 17 knots, the same speed as her sisters.

The ships were remarkably incident-free, a clear reflection of the way they were run and maintained. However, the first season for the *Southend Belle* was marred when the ship was disabled off Felixstowe resulting from a cylinder head blow-out, allegedly due to negligence.

All the newer 'Belle' steamers were characterised by the same basic profile. There was an open Main Deck forward and a long Promenade Deck from the foremast aft; the bridge was between the paddle boxes, they had a single funnel, no mainmast, and all had a bow rudder to assist stern-first work in the Thames and the Orwell. The last three steamers also had identical 105nhp engines, although the dimensions of the vessels themselves varied. The company was reorganised under the title Belle Steamers in 1897, and in mid-season the following year was taken over by hotel and pier owner Coast Development and put under the charge of Mr A. Penfold. Throughout these changes the ships were heavily mortgaged to their builder, William Denny, and the real company assets were surprisingly small.

The paddle boxes of the Belle Steamers fleet were quite distinctive. They had horizontal slats arranged in a series of six columns edged by a white border with star-shaped ports let into it. At the centre of each paddle box was a rising sun surmounted by the arms of the City of London and those of the counties of Essex and Kent.

By the mid-1890s the main Clacton service, operated by the *London Belle*, was advertised to leave Fresh Wharf at 9.30am daily, calling at Southend Pier at 12.15pm for Clacton. A through return fare from Southend to Ipswich in the fore cabin cost 4 shillings, or 5 shillings in the saloon; from Southend to Clacton only was 2 shillings and 2s 6d; and London to Southend returns were 3 shillings and 3s 6d respectively. Timings were brought forward slightly in 1900 with advertised connections at Walton for Southwold and Great Yarmouth as well as Ipswich. Weekend trips from Southend were a popular option and included a night in a company hotel together with a cruise round the Mouse or the Nore Light.

A description of the Belle Steamers, which first appeared in the June 1962 *Sea Breezes*, includes the following on crew income:

'In the early days the crews were able to supplement their meagre wages by hiring out deck chairs. They also sold "hat guards" and in very calm weather business was improved by throwing overboard an old hat to the shout of "Gen'leman's lorst 'is 'at!". Another trick used in some Belles was for one of the crew, pretending to be a passenger, to start ostentatiously throwing coppers at ventilator mouths, always taking care to miss. Passengers soon took up the game with better aim and a bucket under the vent shaft provided the crew with several shillings a trip.'

In 1896 the New Palace Steamers withdrew from the Clacton service, and placed the *Koh-I-Noor* alongside the *Royal Sovereign* on the Margate route. That same year an independent operator started up a Tilbury to Ostend service in direct competition with *La Marguerite* using the former joint Lancashire & Yorkshire and London & North Western Railway's Fleetwood to Belfast ferry *Prince of Wales*, which had just completed a brief spell under the ownership of the Spanish Government. Having proved the viability of the new service, New Palace Steamers was bent on seeing the *Prince of Wales* off the Thames, and a consort for the *La Marguerite* duly arrived at Tilbury in time for the 1897 season. This was *La Belgique*, and as her name suggested she was destined for the Tilbury to Ostend route – there was no longer any sign of the *Prince of Wales* returning.

The *La Belgique* had started her career as the *Paris* on the Newhaven to Dieppe service of the London, Brighton & South Coast Railway in 1875, and was later to end her career in the Western Isles of Scotland as David MacBrayne's *Glendale*. As *La Belgique*, she was registered in the ownership of William Rhodes, an affiliate of Fairfield Shipbuilding & Engineering, and registered locally at Glasgow rather than London. Both William Rhodes and Richard Barnwell, a partner in Fairfield, were registered owners of the *Koh-I-Noor*, *Royal Sovereign* and *La Marguerite* at various times, apparently a mechanism to enable Fairfield Shipbuilding & Engineering to distance itself from the taxable revenue earnings of its ship-owning interests.

As a partner to *La Marguerite*, however, *La Belgique* was found wanting, and was never able to gain the same degree of popularity with the excursionists. Her main drawback was speed, or rather lack of it, since a mere 14 knots was barely adequate for the cross-Channel excursion trade. Besides, her rather outdated compound oscillating engines gave the ship a pulsating surging motion whenever her speed exceeded about 10 knots, providing a feeling that was not overly welcomed by her passengers. *La Belgique* did not reappear in the 1898 season, remaining laid up until she eventually caught the attention of David MacBrayne Limited some five years later; she wore the MacBrayne red and black funnel for only a further three years before she was wrecked off the Mull of Kintyre. From 1898 the Ostend trips were maintained at reduced frequency of twice per week by *La Marguerite*, which also started trips to Calais twice a week, reducing the original Boulogne service from the previous six days per week to just two.

Competition became most intense when both the *Koh-I-Noor* and the *Royal Sovereign* ran the Thanet service for New Palace Steamers towards the end of the century, and Belle Steamers decided to join the fray. GSN also felt threatened, but the market was still able to support all the competitors, although this situation would change once King Edward was on the throne.

One of the familiar sights of the Lower Thames at the turn of the century was that of the rival paddlers belching black coal smoke as they raced between piers to secure their share of passengers waiting at the next pier. A letter to the Editor of *Sea Breezes*, in November 1962, from J. Chambers of Surrey, in response to an earlier article on Belle Steamers, concluded:

'One well-known feature of the Belles was their ability to emit dense clouds of black smoke. At extreme range the larger Belles could be confused with the General Steam Navigation Company's *Eagle* but it was always fairly safe to say that the one belching heavy clouds of smoke was a Belle.'

GSN's *Eagle* was a fine and up-to-date steamer commissioned in 1898. She was designed and built to combat the perceived threat of superior ships in the New Palace Steamers and Belle Steamers fleets. Built by Gourlay Brothers of Dundee, she had some unique features for a Thames steamer, not least that her fore saloon terminated just forward of the foremast (she also originally carried a mainmast). She had a tall thin funnel and, as she was based at Fresh Wharf below London Bridge, there was no need for it to be telescopic. She was just a bit smaller than the *London Belle*, but was finely appointed with full-width saloons fore and aft. The bridge remained in the standard position aft of the funnel and across the paddle boxes. This new steamer put GSN back with the big boys, and was a suitable match for the *Koh-I-Noor* and *Royal Sovereign* as well as the *London Belle*.

The *Eagle* was good for one knot more than the 17-knot *Halcyon* 'classical bird' type of steamer. This was a useful asset on the now highly competitive London to Margate and Ramsgate service. The elderly, and now thoroughly outclassed, reserve steamer *Hoboken* had already been dispatched to the breakers at the end of the 1897 season in anticipation of the arrival in service of the *Eagle*. The latter was well received and quickly became a recognised match for the competition, although *La Marguerite* always remained the firm favourite with the public.

A fresh and long-concealed mystery threat for the 1898 season was under construction on the Clyde by the Clydebank Engineering & Shipbuilding Company, Yard Number 331, which by March 1898 had been given the working name *Mercury*. She had been ordered by Peter Blair Black, proprietor of Planet Steamers, for a new service between Port Victoria, situated on the eastern edge of the Isle of Grain in Kent, and continental ports, in collaboration with the London, Chatham & Dover Railway and in competition with the South Eastern Railway. The *Mercury* had a length of 245 feet and was of heavy build, typical of the Thames excursion steamer. The *Jupiter* was transferred to this route for the 1898 summer season and served also in the summer of 1899, but did not reappear thereafter.

Ultimately, Planet Steamers was unable to complete the funding of the *Mercury*. The Clydebank Engineering & Shipbuilding Company's ledger clearly states that initial outlays on the ship of £4,940 15s 2d remained outstanding

The *Eagle* (1898) off Ramsgate, showing off the fine scrollwork on her bows and with two masts as originally built.

as at 31 March 1898, as the agreed first payment from Black had not been paid. The builders then invited the Glasgow & South Western Railway to consider purchase of the completed vessel as an alternative to ordering a sister to its paddle steamer, (another) *Jupiter*, built for it by J. & G. Thompson in 1896. The minutes of the railway company's Steam Vessels Committee for 28 June 1898 record the inspection of the vessel, then state:

> '...had given instructions for purchase of the steamer for £27,000, on condition that certain alterations were carried out and that the steamer be completed and ready for delivery not later than the 4th proximo – the guaranteed speed to be 18½ knots on a four hour run. It was resolved that the steamer be called *Juno*.'

The *Mercury* project would have been a handsome and worthy addition to the Thames excursion fleets. Two factors conspired against her: one was the near bankruptcy of Planet Steamers and the other was the surprise merger of the London, Chatham & Dover Railway with the South Eastern Railway from 1 January 1899, a move designed to consolidate the weak finances of both companies. Any idea of an unnecessary summer service from Port Victoria to the continent was obviously culled by the railway accountants, and the need for the new steamer was obviated. These factors steered the new ship towards a long career as the dedicated Ayr excursion steamer for the Glasgow & South Western Railway. Incidentally, the builder's balance sheets describe the final costs of the ship as hull £14,075 6s 9d, engines £8,356 14s 2d, and boilers £2,988 17s 7d, which, with a cash-payment boiler inspection of £220, left a profit on sale to the Glasgow & South Western Railway of £1,359 1s 6d.

The Thames *Jupiter*, however, was owned by Mrs Black and not by Planet Steamers. Mrs Black was determined to hold on to her asset, even managing to charter the ship to the Brighton, Worthing & South Coast Steamboat Company during August and September 1900. The *Jupiter* returned from charter to lay up again at London. During her extensive period of retirement, she suffered severe fire damage, and was eventually sold in 1904, briefly serving on the Clyde before being resold for scrap.

The Victoria Steamboat Association ceased

The Clyde steamer *Juno* (1898) seen in London, Midland & Scottish Railway livery as adopted after 1924, looking every bit the likeness of a Thames steamer and spitting image of the slightly enlarged *Golden Eagle* (1909) – see page 86.

trading in 1898. The company had retained the London up-river services and the London piers and Greenwich route since responsibility for the down-river services had been sold in 1894 to New Palace Steamers. At the time, an article in a leading London newspaper described the ageing fleet of little paddle steamers as 'a derelict fleet of floating scrap iron'. Nevertheless, its assets and goodwill were bought by a new company, which began trading under the name Thames Steamboat Company, securing, for the moment, the important local passenger services in and around London. The new company felt sufficiently confident to order three new vessels, and for a while the service looked healthy. At the turn of the century the Thames Steamboat Company had 16 little steamers in operation, each in a neat livery of light green hulls and yellow funnels with narrow black tops. The return fare from London Bridge to Greenwich was sixpence, and the round trip, calling at all piers, took about 90 minutes.

One notable up-river steamer was commissioned in 1895 by Edgar Shand, a new operator. This was the *Queen Elizabeth*, a paddle steamer that had a certificate for a massive 709 passengers for her service from London Bridge to Kew, Richmond and Hampton Court. She subsequently served various owners, but was found unfit for service at the end of the Great War, when she was scrapped.

On the Lower Thames, Belle Steamers had built itself up to be one of the premier excursion operators by the end of the Victorian era, together with New Palace Steamers and the old stalwart GSN. The Medway Steam Packet Company was still waiting quietly in the wings, operating its cross-estuary services. Without the burden of the intense competition suffered by the key operators, the Medway company was able to gain financial strength, a position that could not be achieved either by Belle Steamers or New Palace Steamers, as both were saddled with heavy mortgages against their vessels. GSN, meanwhile, maintained a strong position, not least because it enjoyed cross-subsidy from the company's continental and coastal freight and passenger network. It also maintained a dignity derived from supplying a good and reliable service, provided by well-maintained ships and well-trained and courteous staff.

The excursion network was now at its peak and could only decline in the new century. Sadly the river services had gained a reputation for rowdy

The *Queen Elizabeth* (1895) represented the zenith of the above-bridge fleets, with a capacity for more than 700 passengers.

behaviour, and the irregular licensing arrangements on-shore had given the ships a role as floating drinking-clubs. The problem had become so acute on the Clyde that in 1880 a group of businessmen launched a new excursion company with the purpose-built *Ivanhoe*, on which the ship's bars were conspicuous only by their absence. The *Ivanhoe* led a highly successful career, being popular both with families and with ladies. Rowdy behaviour was never successfully curbed on the longer Thames excursion routes, and it was said that the Foreign Office was relieved at the closure of Eagle Steamers in 1966 as passenger behaviour at Boulogne had given vent to numerous complaints from the French authorities!

Before degeneration of the services set in during the reign of Edward, one interesting development took place at the close of the century using two former cross-Medway ferries that had been commissioned by the South Eastern Railway in 1891. Eric Harrison takes up the tale in an article that first appeared in the October 1967 *Sea Breezes*:

> 'Their names were *Edward William*, after Sir Edward Watkin [Chairman of the South Eastern Railway], and *Myleta**, a somewhat incongruous name. Samuda Brothers built these single-funnelled steamers. They were used at the outset purely for ferry work in the Medway area, running between Sheerness and Port Victoria. However, the 1899 formation of the South Eastern & Chatham Railway rendered such competitive traffic unnecessary so they were unemployed in that season, but in 1900 they were transferred to Folkestone, running summer coastal trips to Dungeness and St Margaret's Bay on alternate weekdays.'

The following year they took up excursions between Folkestone, Dover, Deal and Ramsgate, continuing in service until the end of the 1908 season. The tickets were interchangeable with the rail service, and they proved extremely popular, one starting off at Ramsgate and the other at Folkestone. The success of this new excursion trade enticed the South Eastern & Chatham Railway on to the longer routes on the Thames, making competition even more intense. The old South Eastern Railway had, of course, operated special train and steamer day excursions from London Bridge station via Folkestone to Boulogne since the 1860s and was by no means a newcomer to the excursion trade. However, such additional competition on the Thames routes was unwelcome, and sought only to aggravate commercial pressures on the existing operators.

The *Myleta* and the *Edward William* were sold in 1909 for use at Dubrovnik, renamed *Eva* and *Adam* respectively. In 1911 the *Eva* foundered off the Dardenelles, while the *Adam* was out of register by 1917.

At the close of the century, the halcyon days, at least for the operators, were over, and GSN's own bird of peace and prosperity, the *Halcyon*, was shortly destined for disposal at the tender age of only 17. Before then, in August 1903, she suffered the ignominy of steering gear failure in heavy seas, her passengers being successfully transferred to the *Southwold Belle*, which managed to come alongside. Although the growth years of the Thames excursion steamer fleets were now finished, the great days were still to come. Over-capacity was good for the traveller, who now had unprecedented variety and choice coupled with low and competitive fares. The 1890s may have been the boom years for the excursion companies, but the 1900s were set to be those of the excursionist.

* *Myleta* was named after the granddaughter of Sir Myles Fenton, General Manager of the South Eastern Railway.

6. EDWARDIAN COMPETITION

'The steamers catered for the holiday traffic in a big way; as at holiday times the piers often resembled railway stations; but instead of seeing the modern travelling case of today, cumbersome trunks, valises and a whole paraphernalia of baggage went aboard, having to come off again the other end. At Margate and Ramsgate on the arrival and departure of the steamers, dozens of porters, dressed in smocks, with long barrows trundled the baggage to horse-drawn cabs waiting at the pier entrance, or vice versa. Even with all this, the steamers were emptied and reloaded in less than ten minutes and away, the next following into the berth in its turn.'

H. Collard Stone, *Paddle Wheels*, May 1970

The coronation of King Edward VII in 1901 was followed, of course, by the inevitable Royal Naval Review. Whilst a whole gathering of coastal, cross-Channel and excursion vessels collected at Spithead, the Thames excursion operators sent the *Royal Sovereign*, *Koh-I-Noor*, *Walton Belle*, *Yarmouth Belle* and the little *Cynthia* as their representatives.

The 1900s was set to become a decade of grandeur as the Victorian pretensions began to fall away. Having conquered steam technology (and introduced urban smog along the way!), the Edwardians set about modernising the world – big was most definitely best. But there remained a need for the city dweller to relax and take the fresh sea air, and the demand for the 'butterfly boats' – the excursion ships that came out in the summer and flitted about – was considerable, as the steamers were still the preferred means of transport.

In a space of just 13 years, Belle Steamers had become the premier operator of Thames excursion routes. During the 1890s it had built up a fleet of seven comfortable and well-appointed ships and had the goodwill of a comprehensive network of services. At the turn of the century Belle Steamers was faced with maintaining its supremacy at a time when the trade on offer, although buoyant, was no longer expanding, and when over-capacity was an increasing threat.

In 1901 the competing excursion fleets on the Thames comprised the following:

Belle Steamers: *Clacton Belle*, *Woolwich Belle*, *London Belle*, *Southend Belle*, *Walton Belle*, *Yarmouth Belle* and *Southwold Belle*
New Palace Steamers: *Koh-I-Noor*, *Royal Sovereign* and *La Marguerite*
GSN: *Halcyon*, *Mavis*, *Oriole*, *Laverock*, *Philomel* and *Eagle*
Medway Steam Packet Company: *Lady Margaret* and *Princess of Wales*
Planet Steamers (Messrs P. B. Black): *Jupiter*
Elliot Steam Tug Company: *Conquerer*
William Watkins: *Cynthia*

The main competitors were clearly Belle Steamers, New Palace Steamers and GSN. Each had its own character: the Belle Steamers were considerably upmarket compared with the ageing GSN *Halcyon* 'classical bird' steamers, although the newer *Eagle* had been an attempt to redress this difference. The New Palace Steamers trio stood apart as being both luxurious and fast, and were clearly considered as the market leaders at that time. Both Belle Steamers and New Palace Steamers offered two separate classes of accommodation, and stationed a ticket inspector at the gate between the two classes so that upgrades could be purchased if required. GSN

Above The *Cynthia* (1892) seen in her early days. *National Maritime Museum*

Left The *London Belle* (1893) at Yarmouth.

offered one-class accommodation, which was of intermediate class, reflected also in the fares. Profits were modest – in 1902 GSN grossed £25,200 against expenses of £22,680 for its excursion services. The off-season lay-up at the buoys off Deptford was a considerable drain on expenses and fares were at best competitive in the summer season.

The twin-funnelled tug *Conquerer* was built in 1897 at South Shields and adopted a summer role of excursions from Tilbury to Dover in 1898 and thereafter from Margate and other Lower Thames piers to Folkestone, Calais or Boulogne. Her winters were spent on towing duties. She was a small vessel of only 224 tons gross and remained in service up until the Great War, apparently under a variety of owners including the Elliot Steam Tug Company. After the war she was used in the Channel Islands but was better known as a Forth excursion ship in the mid-1920s, adopting the name *Hurworth* in July 1925 after her sale to the Tees Towing Company, although it did not take delivery of her until the end of the season. The *Conquerer*, however, remains significant as the last passenger steam tug to serve on the Thames.

The Medway Steam Packet Company was largely isolated from competition from the London steamers, cutting its cross-Thames furrow between the Medway ports and Southend. However, catastrophe struck in 1903 when the *Lady Margaret* was gutted by fire while alongside at Rochester. An order was immediately placed with Scott & Company of Kinghorn in Fife for a replacement steamer. The outcome was the

The *City of Rochester* (1904) in the Medway.

magnificent *City of Rochester*, which had cost not only the insurance received against the *Lady Margaret*, but much, much more.

The *City of Rochester* was the company's largest steamer yet. She was equipped with compound diagonal engines, giving her a service speed of 15 knots, and was in every way a modern and efficient steamer with accommodation for 1,000 passengers. Interestingly she was the first Thames estuary steamer to have the bridge placed forward of the funnel, with both bridge and funnel forward of the paddle wheels.

Charles Dance, in an article that first appeared in *Sea Breezes* in September 1978, reported:

> 'For years the forenoon run [to Southend] was well patronised, but the vessel returned fairly empty until someone thought of appointing an agent at Southend. Bills were posted advertising trips to Chatham Dockyard, Upnor and Rochester Castle, with two hours ashore at Rochester, and these were a great success.
>
> In the winter months, engine room staffs and apprentices were put to work overhauling the vessels at the Acorn yard [owned by the company], and deck hands and stokers were found work at Rochester gas works. Foords [the family owners of the company] worked on the principle that if the crew repaired the vessels they sailed in they would make a good job of it. Indeed, the Medway Steam Packet Company was known for its reliable service.
>
> The ships carried a musical trio of harp, violin and clarinet, who paid a weekly fee of 10/- for the privilege. There was a sailing from Strood Pier at 09.15, calling at Chatham, Upnor, Gillingham and Sheerness, then sailing across to Southend, arriving about 11.30am.'

In a surprise move at the close of the 1903 season, Fairfield Shipbuilding & Engineering foreclosed on the mortgage of *La Marguerite* and transferred the big ship from New Palace Steamers to its associate company, the Liverpool & North Wales Steamship Company. There were a number of sound reasons behind this move, and it actually secured the future of the ship as an excursion steamer; she was able to work out of Liverpool right up until the end of the 1925 season. Not least of the difficulties were those encountered by the *Koh-I-Noor*, working from East Coast piers now owned by the Coast Development Company, owners of Belle Steamers. From 1904 the *Koh-I-Noor* forsook the East Coast route and took over some of the duties of *La Marguerite*, when she transferred to London, Margate, Deal and Dover duties. More importantly, *La Marguerite* was able to take up her new duties on the shorter North Wales runs at reduced and more economical speeds, with lower crewing and bunkering costs, which collectively brought the vessel back into profit.

The 1905 season brought with it a new and unforeseen threat. The Dover and Folkestone-based cross-Channel fleet of the South Eastern & Chatham Railway was undergoing revolution with the displacement of its modern fleet of fast paddle steamers by newfangled express turbine steamers, the brainchild of the inventor Sir Charles Parsons. Three turbine steamers – *The Queen*, *Invicta* and *Onward*, built by William Denny – were in service by 1905, and while the French-owned paddle steamers were in full employment, the British ones lay idle for much of the year. The departure of the *La Marguerite* had left a dent in services operated in 1904, and the railway company could see a summer market for its spare steamers.

The *Invicta* (1905), seen in a study of smoke, ran some successful cruises for the South Eastern & Chatham Railway in 1906 and 1907. *National Maritime Museum*

In 1905 the large paddle steamer *Empress* was sent round to Margate to commence a series of daily sailings to Boulogne. The excursions sailed at 10.30am and had trippers back at 7.30 in the evening. Initially three trips were made each week, and at the end of the season the experiment was judged very successful. Although the *Empress* was sold for scrap that winter, services were resumed in 1906 with the paddler *Calais* and the virtually brand-new turbine steamer *Invicta*. The services were extended to include Boulogne, Calais and Dunkirk on most weekdays, with the ships returning to Dover for peak weekend duties.

The *Invicta* and *Calais* were back at Margate in 1907. After that the railway company retreated to its cross-Channel ports, there to provide combined train and steamer day excursions from London as it had long since done and would continue to do for many years to come. These included the Monday-only excursion to Boulogne by the 1898-built paddler *Princess of Wales* (not to be confused with the Medway Steam Packet Company's vessel of the same name), until she was sold out of the railway fleet in 1910, the victim of the turbine steamer. These summer excursions

allowed 10 hours ashore for the price of 6s 6d, while an additional shilling would permit return on the ordinary evening service.

Part of the reason for the withdrawal of the railway steamers from Margate was an aggressive new build for the GSN. This was the turbine steamer *Kingfisher*, which had arrived on the Thames from William Denny's shipyard at Dumbarton in time for the 1906 season. The contract price of the new ship was £36,968, of which £13,741 was committed to her turbine machinery – the builder's model of the steamer can be inspected to this day at the National Maritime Museum. Like the *Invicta*, she was driven by three direct-drive turbines connected to three separate shafts. While the *Invicta* was designed with a service speed of 21 knots, the *Kingfisher* was good for just over 20 knots. The new excursion ship was luxuriously appointed with first class accommodation only, and her Promenade Deck was plated right up to her bows. She took up service based at Tilbury, to Southend, Margate, Ramsgate and Deal, followed by either a trip across the Channel to Boulogne or a coastal cruise, which from 1907 included a call at Dover. However, her first season was beset by technical problems with her turbines, which had also delayed her delivery from the Clyde.

The arrival of the *Kingfisher* allowed the first of the *Halcyon* quintet to be disposed of; none of them had electric lighting and were all now quite dated. While the *Halcyon* had earlier spent part of the 1894 season under charter to operators at Hastings, it was no surprise that she was sold to them for service during the 1905 season. Serious competition from P. & A. Campbell forced the withdrawal of the *Halcyon* at the end of that season, when she had to be returned to GSN for non-payment of instalments; she was later sold for use on the Elbe.

It was apparent that the remaining vessels of the *Halcyon* class were not up to the grand expectations of the Edwardian excursionists. The *Philomel* was sold in 1907, followed by the *Laverock* in 1908, and the *Mavis* in 1909. The *Philomel* went to the Furness Railway at Barrow, where the good citizens always referred to her as the 'Full-o-Smell'. The *Laverock* went to new owners in Bordeaux,

The turbine steamer *Kingfisher* (1906) seen at Dover; she survived only five seasons on the Thames. *DP World P&O Heritage Collection*

The *Laverock* (1889) was the third of the 'classical bird' quintet to be sold.

and the *Mavis* to Pockett's Bristol Channel Steam Packet, where she was soon declared uneconomical. The *Mavis* was sold for scrap at the start of the First World War, her parts being more valuable to the war effort than the prospect of her conversion to a minesweeper.

The compensation for these three disposals was the wonderful *Golden Eagle*. This paddle steamer was everything that the turbine steamer *Kingfisher* was not. She was manoeuvrable at the exposed piers of the estuary, she could get up to speed and slow down rapidly; above all, with a speed of 19 knots driven by triple-expansion engines, she was economical. Her overall size was broadly similar to that of the *Kingfisher*, although she was 25 feet shorter than the *Royal Sovereign*.

The *Golden Eagle* was built by John Brown at Clydebank, the successor to the Clydebank Engineering & Shipbuilding Company that had previously worked on the *Mercury* project for the Victoria Steamboat Association. It is no surprise, therefore, to learn that the *Golden Eagle* was basically an enlarged version of what had become the Glasgow & South Western Railway's excursion steamer *Juno*. The *Juno*, of course, had originally been intended for service from the Thames to Margate and continental ports under

The *Golden Eagle* (1909) was an attractive addition to the GSN fleet. *George Robins collection*

the auspices of the Victoria Steamboat Association and Planet Steamers (see Chapter 5). Unlike the innovative *City of Rochester*, the *Golden Eagle* retained the bridge across the paddles behind the single large funnel, while the Promenade Deck led from the bows almost to the stern.

The *Golden Eagle* was placed on the Fresh Wharf to Margate and Ramsgate run, displacing the *Eagle*, which now took up service from Tilbury to Southend, Margate, Ramsgate, Deal and Dover. Sailings from Southend Pier to the Thanet ports in 1909 were as follows (ie in addition to the Belle Steamers daily 12.00 sailing to Clacton and second steamer for Yarmouth plus weekend relief sailings, and also the services of the Medway Steam Packet Company):

Mondays and Thursdays

10.30 *Kingfisher* to Margate and Boulogne
10.30 *Eagle* to Margate, Ramsgate and Dover
11.00 *Koh-I-Noor* to Margate, Ramsgate, Deal and Dover
11.30 *Golden Eagle* to Margate and Ramsgate
11.50 *Royal Sovereign* to Margate and Ramsgate
12.00 Belle Steamer to Margate and Ramsgate

Tuesdays

10.30 *Eagle* to Margate, Ramsgate and Dover
11.30 *Golden Eagle* to Margate and Ramsgate
11.00 *Koh-I-Noor* to Margate, Ramsgate, Deal and Dover
11.50 *Royal Sovereign* to Margate and Ramsgate
12.00 Belle Steamer to Margate and Ramsgate

Wednesdays

10.30 *Kingfisher* to Margate and Dover
11.00 *Koh-I-Noor* to Margate, Ramsgate, Deal and Dover
11.30 *Golden Eagle/Eagle* to Margate and Ramsgate
11.50 *Royal Sovereign* to Margate and Ramsgate
12.00 Belle Steamer to Margate and Ramsgate

Fridays

10.30 *Kingfisher* to Margate and Dover
11.30 *Golden Eagle/Eagle* to Margate and Ramsgate

Saturdays

10.30 *Kingfisher* to Margate
11.00 *Koh-I-Noor* to Margate and Ramsgate
11.30 *Golden Eagle* to Margate and Ramsgate
11.30 *Eagle* to Margate and Ramsgate as relief
11.50 *Royal Sovereign* to Margate and Ramsgate
12.00 Belle Steamer to Margate and Ramsgate

Sundays

11.00 *Koh-I-Noor* to Margate, Ramsgate, Deal and Dover
11.45 *Kingfisher* to Margate and Dover
11.50 *Royal Sovereign* to Margate and Ramsgate
12.00 Belle Steamer to Margate and Ramsgate
12.10 *Golden Eagle* to Margate and Ramsgate
12.10 *Eagle* to Margate and Ramsgate as relief

The early Saturday sailings gave up to 7 hours ashore, while both the *Kingfisher* and *Koh-I-Noor* returned for the 'Husband's Boat' service with

The *Southwold Belle* (1900) with a full load of Edwardian trippers.

From 'London Bridge Below' by R. Austin-Freeman, in *Living London*, a three-volume Edwardian pictorial, date and publisher not stated

'Close on the left as we pass through the Bridge is Fresh Wharf, that famous rendezvous of the London trippers, and the pier barges are even now gay with their somewhat bizarre costumes, for a couple of steamers lie alongside bound respectively for Ramsgate and Walton-on-the-Naze. As we watch the warning bell from the outer boat begins to ring furiously, occasioning a general stampede on the pier.

Flannel-trousered youths in nautical peaked caps, accompanied by young women in white dresses, with shoes and stockings to match, bustle on board, and presently finding that they are in the wrong boat, bustle back again. Stout, red-faced women drag protesting children up and down the pier, and a belated musician, encumbered with a harp, gets jammed in the gangway and has to be extricated by an attendant fiddler.

Then the bell stops, the rattling steam capstans wind in the shore ropes, and the whistle emits an exultant war whoop. The vessel glides away amidst a cloud of black smoke and a burst of harmony from the musicians on the saloon deck.'

From *Thames Pleasures and Sports* by John Bloundelle-Burton

'There is always a band on board (harp, cornet and flute), refreshments may be obtained, all are determined in enjoying themselves, and lovers are abundant and shed a rosy glow around. In the case of the "husband's boat" – for Margate on Saturdays – it is the married men hastening to join their wives until Monday, who represent the votaries of Hymen, late Cupid; yet they are happy...'

connecting train from Fenchurch Street to Tilbury and sailing direct to Margate. The *Southwold Belle* took the only London to Margate (via Tilbury) 'Husband's Boat' service, leaving Fresh Wharf at 2.00pm. The rail and sea journeys were interchangeable on the *Southwold Belle*, the return fare being 6 shillings in the saloon and 5 shillings in the fore cabin.

The Dover sailings by the *Eagle* only commenced in 1909, as the excursion tug *Conquerer* had then ceased her daily run from Tilbury to Dover and back. The *Conquerer*, under the command of Captain Wash, had then adopted the Margate to Dover and Folkestone service as replacement for the *Myleta* and *Edward William*, which had been withdrawn by their owner, the South Eastern & Chatham Railway, the previous year (see Chapter 4).

The *Kingfisher* meanwhile retained her duties on the Tilbury to Boulogne service, reputedly assisting the murderer Dr Crippen to flee the country, while the sole survivor of the *Halcyon* class, the *Oriole*, was retained in reserve until sold in 1912. Although the *Kingfisher* had been successful in seeing off the competition from the South Eastern & Chatham Railway, she was not consistently successful in breaking even. Her hull design was such that there was a constant queue of boat people demanding compensation for upsets in her wake in the Channel above Canvey Island. Much like the Stena HSS ferries in Belfast Lough, the *Kingfisher* was obliged to crawl along the reaches below Tilbury until the Channel widened sufficiently for the turbines to be pressured up to a useful speed. In the Channel itself the ship was reportedly stiff in a head sea and liable to roll, sometimes alarmingly, especially when the waves were on her beam. As time went on she became less popular with excursionists, who preferred the traditional stability of the paddle steamer.

The year 1911 brought some shocks: with King George V now on the throne the withdrawal of both the *Kingfisher* and the *Southwold Belle* was a sad ending to the Edwardian era. The *Kingfisher*, in hindsight, was an admission by GSN of the unsuitability of its turbine steamer to the duties of the excursion trade. Too big for excursions, too small for cross-Channel work, it was sensible to sell the vessel while a good price could be had for her. In 1912 she took up her new life in Trieste as the *Venezia*, and survived in service until 1938. 1911 was also the year when a brave ship's carpenter, Richard Bell, jumped from the *Golden Eagle* in mid-Channel to rescue a passenger who had fallen overboard.

The withdrawal of the *Southwold Belle* was due to two factors: increased capacity caused by the arrival of the *Golden Eagle* and the fact that Belle Steamers was not doing so well. That the newest of the 'Belles' should be put up for sale again reflected favourable prices for that class, complete with triple-expansion engines and steel floats, and age of ship. That she had to be sold at all was due to loss of traffic to the *Golden Eagle*, a fickle public preferring to travel if at all possible on the newest and the best. The sale price of the *Southwold Belle* enabled the company to pay off its debts, not least to the coal merchants on whom it was so dependent. With her bridge finally moved forward of the funnel, she was sold to HAPAG for use as a tender, initially at Hamburg. Thereafter she had a variety of owners before being scrapped in 1925.

With the *Southwold Belle* gone, the sheltered existence of the *Woolwich Belle* had to come to an end and she was converted from the River Orwell steamer to a fully-fledged sea-going pleasure ship ready for the 1912 season. The Orwell service was left in the hands of the Great Eastern Railway's double-ended paddle steamers *Suffolk* and *Norfolk*, the *Essex* being sold in 1913 for use on the Thames (see Chapter 4).

The *Woolwich Belle* lost her telescopic funnel back in the early 1900s in favour of a new one-piece fixed funnel. Then in the winter of 1911/12 she was stripped and partially rebuilt such that her Upper Deck was extended to the mast and the saloon was made full-width. She was given a slightly broader funnel in the 1920s. At the same time the *Clacton Belle* was given two additional lifeboats, which were slung on davits on the Fore Deck. She carried these only until 1914 when they were removed.

This, then, was the position as Europe drifted towards war to close what had been an idyllic era

The last of the Great Eastern Railway excursion steamers to be built for the Ipswich to Felixstowe service was the *Norfolk* (1900).

The *Woolwich Belle* (1891) as modified for estuarine work in the late 1900s, with a forward saloon that was added in 1912. *Bob Drewett collection*

of grand ideals coupled with unstinting support for the excursion steamers. This was the end of the golden era, with the magnificent flagship of the Thames, the *Golden Eagle*, at one end of the spectrum, and the little *Woolwich Belle* at the other. It was also a period fêted with long warm summers that suited the business of the 'butterfly boats' perfectly. But the Edwardians, it might be added, for all their engineering skills, had still not overcome one of the London river's age-old problems, as reported by Eric Thornton in his book *Thames Coast Pleasure Steamers*:

> '... from the passengers' point of view, probably the greatest nuisance of the river trip was when the vessel had to punch against a flood tide all the way from London Bridge when the effluent from the sewers was carried up river.'

Before leaving the marvellous and heady days of the early part of the century, mention must be made of one of the grandest Edwardian ideas, which in reality was none other than political nonsense. This is the glorious story of London County Council, which voted in the idea of running the London Pier river services itself following the withdrawal of the London Steamboat Company from 1902.

During 1904 and 1905 a fleet of 30 (yes, 30!) near-identical paddle steamers was constructed for the Council at a cost of around £6,000 each by the Thames Ironworks, J. I. Thorneycroft & Company at Woolston, Napier & Miller at Glasgow and G. Rennie at Greenwich. And what bonny little boats they were: compound diagonal engines drove them at 12 knots, and with a gross tonnage of between 116 and 125 tons they could carry 530 passengers. Although the Promenade Deck was open there was a large awning aft to protect passengers from the vagaries of the London weather, and there was a comfortable lounge on the Main Deck.

Frank Burtt takes up the story in *Steamers of the Thames and Medway*:

> 'Realising the relief it would give to road traffic congestion, the Council again applied for the necessary powers [having already been turned down in 1902]. These were obtained in 1904 and a service was started on 17 June 1905, between Hammersmith and Greenwich with a fleet of 30 steamboats, HRH The Prince of Wales inaugurating the service on the *King Alfred*. The boats were worked on such a heavy loss that they were taken off in October 1907, and on 15

The London County Council steamers *Marlowe* (1905), built by G. Rennie & Company of Greenwich (*above*) and the *Raleigh* (1905), built by J. I. Thornycroft & Company, Southampton, and showing subtly different interpretations of the design plans.

Woe betide any excursion steamer that got to windward of the cattle boat *Claud Hamilton* (1875)!

December 1907 the Council decided to sell the 30 boats and invited tenders for their purchase. The total deficiency for the three years working was £162,499. The London County Council disposed of 14 boats to a new concern called the City Steamboat Company [at a cost of £393 each], which worked a 10-minute service from 1909 until August 1914, when the service stopped for the outbreak of war. The other boats were distributed far and wide.'

The Council achieved only two things – the removal of all competition on the river and the cessation of the winter service from 1909 onwards. Its bizarre action did, however, provide a glut of little steamers, some surviving in service until the late 1930s. Norman Cox described the affair in an article that first appeared in *The Illustrated London News* of January 1971:

'So the London County Council stepped in like inexperienced weekend sailors. A heavy-handed attitude soon antagonised the smaller companies. Their strong challenge was supported by a deep pocket. They built 30 steamers to carry 500 passengers in each. They built new piers, and employed Captain Arthur Owen, formerly master of *La Marguerite*, as an adviser. With typical muddled bureaucracy, they then built the London tram system and put their own river service out of business.'

There were also two cattle boats owned by the Corporation of London. These were used to tranship cattle arriving in the big freighters from America that moored off Gravesend to the Deptford Foreign Cattle Market. The boats were the *Racoon*, built originally for G. & J. Burns's Glasgow to Belfast service in 1868, and the *Claud Hamilton*, one-time crack steamer of the Harwich Continental services of the Great Eastern Railway and launched by and named after the company Chairman in 1875. But it was the curse of the day trip should a returning excursion steamer fall in behind one of the cattle boats at Gravesend, especially against an ebb tide on a still summer's evening!

7. THE FIRST WORLD WAR AND ITS AFTERMATH

'[The *Golden Eagle*] and twenty other GSN vessels were requisitioned by the Admiralty and deployed on various duties, the *Golden Eagle* being converted to a seaplane carrier at one time and carrying some 518,000 troops and other units. In all GSN lost 23 vessels on active service.'

From an article by Alan Peake, *Lloyd's Log*, 1974

King George V had been on the throne for only four years before events in Europe slid towards all-out war. By 4 August 1914 Britain had declared war on Germany following Germany's declaration against Russia and France and the German invasion of Belgium. In the fond hope that the war would all be over by Christmas, life in some quarters carried on as normal, at least for a while.

There was an immediate ban on excursion steamers going beyond Southend and Margate. This reflected both the likelihood of mines in the Thames approaches and the large naval presence centred on Dover harbour. While some ships were immediately withdrawn, others saw the season through; the *Koh-I-Noor*, for example, was at once withdrawn and dispatched to the Clyde for reboilering, but the *Royal Sovereign* continued until the end of her normal season (minus Ramsgate calls) before retiring to Tilbury Basin.

The *Koh-I-Noor* and the *Royal Sovereign* both had a peaceful war. The large window areas along their Main Decks deemed them unsuitable for conversion to an aggressive role, and as reboilering the *Koh-I-Noor* was not a war priority the steamer was sent to lay up in Gareloch while her sister languished at Tilbury.

The 'Belle' steamers continued to operate through August and into September, as did the *Golden Eagle*. The *Eagle*, however, like the *Koh-I-Noor*, was withdrawn from service and laid up in the docks, later to be converted for minesweeping duties. The first of the steamers to be requisitioned was the *Golden Eagle*, which took up trooping duties early in 1915, reportedly carrying over 500,000 troops across the Channel. Here she often worked alongside *La Marguerite*, which carried more than 360,000 troops, mainly from Southampton, under her civilian master Captain John Young.

The First World War was the last great infantry war, but it was also a maritime war. Britain lost 9 million tons of shipping in the ensuing four years of conflict, during which new and deadly weapons were deployed, including the submarine and various types of mines. The shallow draft of paddle steamers was immediately in great demand – they provided almost the perfect floating platforms for use as minesweepers. One by one the little steamers took up military service under the title His Majesty's Paddle Mine Sweeper:

Clacton Belle (as HMPMS 930), August 1915 to December 1919
Yarmouth Belle (as HMPMS 929), August 1915 to January 1920
Eagle (as HMS *Aiglon*/HMPMS 938), December 1915 to July 1920
Walton Belle (as HMPMS 579/HC 3), December 1915 to May 1919
London Belle (as HMPMS 530/HC 2), March 1916 to April 1919
Southend Belle (as HMPMS 532), April 1916 to November 1919

Above The *Clacton Belle* (1890) as HMPMS 930 on active service.

Below HMS *Totnes* (1916), one of 32 minesweepers of the *Ascot* class. Mined in December 1916, her forepart was rebuilt and she was put back in service, but was scrapped in 1922.

When HMPMS 579 fished up a new type of German mine in the Thames estuary it was thereafter always referred to as the 'Walton Belle Mine'. She was moved north to the Tyne later in the war. The Thames steamers were comparatively lucky, none being lost on active service, although some of their counterparts from the South Coast did not survive.

So successful were the paddle minesweepers that the Admiralty built and commissioned a fleet of 32 such vessels, based on the design of the *Glen Usk*, which had only been completed in 1914 for P. & A. Campbell's Bristol Channel excursion services. The ships were 246 feet long, and had distinctive cruiser sterns. They also had widely spaced funnels as they had two separate boiler rooms, one forward and one aft of the engine room. The fleet became the *Ascot* class of paddle minesweepers, all the ships being named after racecourses. Five were lost in the war, one was sold and the remaining 26 were laid up for several years after hostilities ceased (see Chapter 8).

The smallest member of the 'Belle' fleet, the *Woolwich Belle*, never left the Thames during the war, and, serving as a stores ship, rarely left the London Dock system. Like that stay-at-home ship,

The Mersey ferry *Iris* (1906) partnered sister ship *Daffodil* (1906) in the Zeebrugge raids, after which the pair were awarded their 'Royal' prefixes; the *Royal Daffodil* was later destined to bring her name into the New Medway company fleet in 1934.

the Medway Steam Packet Company's *Princess of Wales* and *City of Rochester* rarely left the Medway. The *Princess of Wales* was requisitioned from her normal ferry and tender duties in June 1917 and given the name *Padua*, although she remained on duty in the Medway area. Both the *Padua* and the *City of Rochester* played a vital role in supporting the preparation of the blockships lying off the Nore Light preparatory to the raid on the Zeebrugge Canal in April 1918. It was this raid that earned the two Mersey Ferries *Iris* and *Daffodil* (see Chapter 9) the titles *Royal Iris* and *Royal Daffodil* by command of the King for their part in the raid alongside HMS *Vindictive*.

The *City of Rochester* did stray to the Irish Sea for a brief period, operating as a minesweeper. She very nearly became a casualty back in the Medway, having been tied up alongside the minelayer *Princess Irene* at Sheerness on 27 May 1915, just before the latter was destroyed by a devastating explosion. As the fireball subsided, pieces of the former three-funnelled coastal liner, newly built for the Canadian Pacific Steamship Company, flew far and wide, a section of her boilers apparently landing in Sittingbourne some 9km distant. Although the *City of Rochester* was considerably damaged in the blast, she was able to proceed upstream under her own power to Chatham. She was finally released from duty in November 1919, while the *Padua* was allowed to return to her civilian name and duties only in April 1920. Other wartime tenders on the Medway included the former Scottish pleasure steamers *Roslin Castle* and *Strathmore*.

The Armistice was signed in November 1918, and the peace treaty of Versailles in June 1919. The Britain that emerged from those terrible years had been thoroughly ravaged by the demands of war. Not only had the country lost a large part of a generation of young men, but it returned to civilian life to face the Spanish flu epidemic, a deadly type of bird flu virus that targeted both the very young and the very old. Materials were scarce, jobs were poorly paid, and although the country was set for a post-war boom, the early post-war years were hard indeed.

Happily, all the Thames excursion steamers and many of their crews had survived. However, in 1919 the *London Belle* and *Walton Belle* were dispatched to the White Sea via Norway's North Cape as the hospital tenders HC *2* and HC *3*. There they assisted the expedition against the Bolsheviks in North Russia, supported by the Allies ostensibly to stem the spread of communism. Although the two little paddle steamers demonstrated admirable sea-going qualities, they were not much used on arrival apart from deploying landing parties, during which snipers' bullets pock-marked their funnels and ventilators. There were a number of casualties during these raids but the ships performed admirably. The HC *3* was at one time captured by the Bolshevik army, but was retaken by an engineer officer from a British merchant ship in the area, who rallied the crew and regained possession. The two ships later returned to the Thames, taking three weeks to complete the journey, and were finally released by the Admiralty in May 1920. Not quite so lucky were the two former Forth excursion steamers *Edinburgh Castle* and *Lord Morton*, which had also been dispatched as hospital tenders only to be blown up in September 1919 in order to avoid capture by the Russia Bolsheviks.

Unhappily, both the Coast Development Corporation, owners of Belle Steamers, and New Palace Steamers went out of business during the war. They were finally brought down by arrears in shipbuilders' mortgages at a time when passenger fares were not forthcoming and when mean Government charter fees barely paid to feed even the rats in the bilges. The Medway Steam Packet Company also ceased to exist, as Charles Dance explains, in *Sea Breezes*, September 1978:

> 'On 12 March 1917, Thomas Foord died and the original Medway Steam Packet Company came to an end. The family is remembered in Rochester by the fine almshouses at Priestfields. In December 1919, the New Medway Steam Packet Company was incorporated by Captain S. J. Shippick, the new Managing Director, a master mariner with deep sea experience. He had sailed pleasure steamers from Bournemouth before 1914. The new company carried on as before, retaining the services of the Manager, Mr E. H. Elliot, and the Chief Engineer, Mr R. B. Wills.'

Not only were the people tired from their military effort, but so too were the ships, all being in desperate need of rehabilitation and repair. Only one pleasure steamer was operating on the Thames in 1919. This was the *Royal Sovereign*, awoken from her slumbers at Tilbury, her brass polished, her engines quickly overhauled, and able to take up duties from Old Swan Pier to Margate in May 1919. As the mortgage payments to the Fairfield Shipbuilding & Engineering Company for both the *Royal Sovereign* and the *Koh-I-Noor* could not be paid by New Palace Steamers while the ships were inactive during the war, the shipbuilders reclaimed the two vessels. The *Koh-I-Noor*, with a faded yellow and rust-streaked funnel, abandoned for so long in Gareloch and still in need of new boilers, was dispatched in 1918 to Thomas W. Ward at Morecambe to realise her scrap value, some £6,200.

The *Royal Sovereign*, which had earlier received new boilers in 1909, was sold for £8,300 to the newly formed Royal Sovereign Steamship Company under the directorship of Mr A. W. Pickard. It was this company that had the ship prepared for the 1919 season. However, this process bankrupted it, and it was reconstituted in May 1919 under the same name, but with additional funds provided by three new partners who joined Mr Pickard, the brothers Messrs Shankland and Shankland and a Mr de Mathos. With the Thames entirely to herself, the *Royal Sovereign* provided a much-needed service that earned the new company useful financial recompense in that first season. Additional cash was forthcoming when the *Royal Sovereign* was put on a commuter service during a rail strike in early October, leaving Southend at 6.30am and returning from Old Swan Pier at 4.00pm, with calls en route at Woolwich.

Belle Steamers also needed new owners and an influx of cash. The Coast Development Corporation had been placed in the hands of Receivers, Whinney, Smith & Whinney, in 1915, being in debt to shipbuilder William Denny for much the same reasons that New Palace Steamers had also failed. Denny took the *Woolwich Belle* as a one-off settlement of the outstanding mortgage debt and set about refurbishing her at its yard in Dumbarton. The yard was short of work at this time and the work on the *Woolwich Belle* was helpful towards key worker retention and employment. The work was completed ready for her sale to Channel Excursion Steamers for use at Brighton, with the name *Queen of the South*, in time for the 1922 season.

Whinney, Smith & Whinney had the *London Belle* and *Walton Belle* refurbished ready for the 1920 season. These vessels had already been converted from minesweepers to hospital support vessels and the conversion work needed to return them to passenger duties was not extensive. The pair was chartered to Mr Kingsman of Clacton, who had the *London Belle* back on the London to Walton service and the *Walton Belle* on Yarmouth to Walton duties. Also in 1920 GSN was able to reinstate the *Golden Eagle* on the London to Ramsgate service, and the reconstituted New Medway Steam Packet Company resumed civilian services on Medway ferry and Southend services. The *Royal Sovereign* continued and was allowed to extend to Ramsgate for the season. Vessels still to be refurbished or still on active duty were the *Eagle*, *Clacton Belle*, *Southend Belle* and *Yarmouth Belle*, though all were ready to resume civilian life in time for the 1921 season.

With the return of all the steamers to service in 1921, the pickings were not good, wages were low and Britain was now suffering a short-lived depression before the economy again picked up. GSN was aloof from the short-term losses of this period, being cross-subsidised by its numerous buoyant home trade cargo and passenger routes. The New Medway Steam Packet Company, under the firm management of an astute Captain Shippick, cut its cloth appropriately and stuck out the lean years.

Perhaps surprisingly, given the conditions, Mr Kingsman undertook to buy the Coast Development Corporation and its goodwill from its Receivers toward the end of the 1921 season. Selling all the piers except Clacton to local companies, Mr Kingsman was left with the five 'Belle' steamers, their upkeep, dues and wages. However, he was not encumbered for long as another new company, the PSM Syndicate, hove alongside in October 1921 and bought the five remaining steamers, leaving Mr Kingsman with just Clacton Pier to his name. But just who was the PSM Syndicate? It was none other than Messrs Pickard, Shankland, Shankland and de Mathos from the reconstituted Royal Sovereign Steamship Company.

Thus in 1922 the situation was as follows:

GSN: *Golden Eagle* and *Eagle* operating London to Southend, Margate and Ramsgate

Belle Steamers (operated by PSM Syndicate): *Clacton Belle*, *Southend Belle*, *Walton Belle* and *Yarmouth Belle* on London to Walton, Yarmouth to Walton and London to Ramsgate, with *London Belle* inoperative for season in order to save cash

Royal Sovereign Steamship Company: *Royal Sovereign* on London to Margate and Ramsgate

New Medway Steam Packet Company: *Princess of Wales*, *City of Rochester* on Medway ports and Southend services and *Audrey* under refurbishment at company's Acorn yard

The *Audrey* was only released from Admiralty service back to Captain Shippick in July 1922. The arrival of this former Bournemouth-based vessel in the Medway fleet was the precursor to a substantial expansion of the New Medway Steam Packet Company. Charles Dance takes up the story again:

> 'One of the steamers Captain Shippick had operated at Bournemouth in 1914 was the *Audrey*, serving Studland, Swanage and Poole. Built by Armstrong Whitworth & Company in 1897 for the Tyne General Ferry Company, she was a vessel of 203 tons gross. Sold to Irish owners, Captain Shippick bought her from them, and in the early part of the war sailed her from Poole to Chatham and chartered her to the Admiralty. At this time Captain T. J. Aldis DSC joined the company and became Shippick's right-hand man. Between them they built up and expanded the New Medway company until it became generally known as "Shippick's Navy".'

Captain Sydney G. Shippick had previously been mate of Cosens's excursion steamer *Majestic* at Bournemouth and had served as relief master on its steamers *Empress* and *Victoria*. In 1912 Captain Shippick left Cosens to buy the small steamer *Advance*, which he brought to Bournemouth and put on the Boscombe to Studland ferry as the *Studland Belle*. This wooden-hulled clinker-built steamer was gutted by fire two winters later, and it was for this reason that the slightly larger steamer *Audrey* had been acquired by Shippick.

At the end of the 1922 season Mr Kingsman,

Above Captain Sydney Shippick's first vessel was the little *Studland Belle* (1904), which served the Boscombe to Studland ferry from 1912 to 1914 before being gutted by fire.

Below Captain Shippick's all-time favourite was the little *Audrey* (1897), which was originally designed for ferry duties on the Tyne and was bought to replace the *Studland Belle*. It was the *Audrey* that joined Shippick at Rochester in 1923.

proprietor of Clacton Pier, foreclosed on the PSM Syndicate's mortgage and again became the owner of Belle Steamers. That winter he was able to bolster his bank account when he sold the goodwill and assets of the Belle Steamers outright to new owners. That the new owners should comprise Messrs Pickard, Shankland, Shankland and de Mathos under the banner of the Royal Sovereign Steamship Company should surprise nobody, but somebody somewhere was clearly in profit, although it is not at all apparent who that was! The financial shenanigans continued through to 1925 when the assets of the Royal Sovereign Steamship Company were divided. The RS Steamship Company became the owners of the *Royal Sovereign* and *London Belle*, and the East Anglia Steamship Company, with Mr R. Shankland as Managing Director, became the owners of the *Clacton Belle*, *Southend Belle*, *Walton Belle* and *Yarmouth Belle*.

It had taken four years for the excursion services to get back on their feet as revenue-earning enterprises after the war. Bankruptcy, receivership, sale and resale had been the order of the day, with two vessels, the *Koh-I-Noor* and the *Woolwich Belle*, gone and just one new arrival, the little *Audrey*, yet to take up service. The devastation of war had seen the demise of both New Palace Steamers and Belle Steamers, once the main contenders on the Thames. GSN had come through relatively unscathed and operated the only modern, large luxury steamer on the river, the *Golden Eagle*. However, the infant New Medway Steam Packet Company was all set to give GSN a run for its money, while the pre-war competitors continued to be tossed from one owner to the next, season by season, with little apparent regard to the needs of the excursionist.

Insight into the rigours of coal-fired steamers was given by W. G. Peak (later Managing Director of the New Medway Steam Packet Company) in an article that first appeared in *Paddle Wheels*, Summer 1975. It describes his time as second engineer aboard the *Eagle* in the 1923 season:

> 'On an average day she consumed 25 tons of coal and had to bunker every night. In this particular season, the *Eagle* commenced from Greenwich Pier at 8.00am and was excursion boat to Margate via Woolwich and Southend and then an afternoon sea trip from Margate. We used to arrive back at Deptford buoys about 10.00pm and open up again at 05.00am for washing down, etc. During the night period the coal barge would come alongside and a gang of coalies would walk the 25 tons of coal in sacks aboard round the alleyways. The night firemen would clean all fires of clinker and heave it up from the stokehold and dump it in the ash barge. All this noise and clatter while we were trying to snatch a few hours precious sleep in the cabins below.
>
> After the coalies had finished, usually about 5.00am, the alleyways, engines, etc, were all covered with coal dust and the amount of cleaning necessary was enormous. What a difference when oil firing came along!'

The *Eagle* had been reboilered just before the war, but as her new boilers were heavier than the old pair she sat lower in the water. At full speed this tended to choke the paddle boxes with water. Extra power was needed to maintain speed, and apparently the water in the boilers would get quite turbulent, making the correct reading of the level in the gauge glasses quite difficult. In August 1924 both the ticket collector and master of the *Eagle* were censored for overcrowding – the hand click counter was yet to be invented!

Given the problems of coal and steam, a new development was taking place that would have important repercussions for the excursion fleets. This was the introduction of the internal combustion engine to passenger traffic. Pioneered in passenger ships by David MacBrayne in the Western Highlands before the Great War, the oil engine (and before that the paraffin engine) had begun to find favour with owners of small harbour craft and with some liner operators, notably the Glen Line and Elder Dempster. The pioneering cross-Channel motor ships of the Belfast Steamship Company and the DFDS North Sea fleet were yet to be conceived, but two very early purpose-built motor excursion vessels were commissioned for the Thames, demonstrating once and for all the viability of the motor ship in the excursion trade.

The first was the twin-engined motor ship *New Prince of Wales*, which was built by John I.

The twin-funnelled *Southend Britannia* (1924) sets out from the jetty at Southend with a full load.

Thorneycroft & Company for the newly formed Southend Motor Navigation Company in 1923 at a cost of £11,000, with funding from local businessmen W. H. Wilson and Albert Brand. She was a small, flat-bottomed, wooden-hulled vessel of just 137 tons gross, but had a comfortable saloon on the Lower Deck situated between a pair of narrow outside alleyways. Catering was of a high standard. She was normally employed on short cruises from the company's own jetty to the east of the pier, just beyond the Kursaal funfair adjacent to what was the Jolly Boys. Her roster depended on the tide, giving her a 4-hour window normally enabling two 2-hour cruises. During low-tide periods she operated from a shore-side berth at the pier head. Her paraffin engines gave her a cruising speed of 13 knots, although she could make more than 15 knots when pressed. Remarkably, when fully loaded she drew only 3 feet of water.

The second was the slightly larger *Southend Britannia*, completed in 1924, again by John I. Thorneycroft, this time for Messrs Charles & Arthur Myall, also of Southend. She was of 147 gross tons and carried an impressive two funnels and two masts, a veritable pocket liner. She was also confined to tide-dependent local cruises and had a licence to carry 400 passengers. The Myalls also operated from their own jetty, which was about 50 yards west of the Southend Motor Navigation Company's jetty offshore of the old Boating Lake (now Adventure Island Amusements). Competition between the *Southend Britannia* and the *New Prince of Wales* was intense, but the ships were normally well patronised, their owners cashing in on the fact that other sea cruises started a mile and a half away down the far end of the pier, save for days when a low tide forced the two stalwarts down to the end of the pier as well. Both ships had bow rudders to help backing away from the beach, and both had twin rudders.

8. CAPTAIN SHIPPICK'S NAVY

By 1923 the New Medway Steam Packet Company, with Captain Sydney G. Shippick in the post of Managing Director, was on the lookout for new tonnage with which to expand its routes. In an article in *Paddle Wheels*, Winter 1974, H. Collard Stone explained why expansion was essential for the company:

> 'Whilst the old company, with the *City of Rochester*, 235 gross tons, speed 14 knots, and *Princess of Wales*, 163 gross tons, capable of little over 11 knots, had maintained this service, styled "The Voyage of Variety" between the Medway towns and Southend, which they and their predecessors had done for many years, the new company was about to embark on a policy of expansion, opening up new routes, as additional shipping tonnage became available to them. Captain Shippick, very much alive to the changing conditions of the post-war era, which was already in evidence, especially with the motor coach taking traffic away from the steamboats, and with his weather eye on the London operators, was aware of the necessity of breaking away from the old traditions.
>
> Herne Bay, ripe as the first objective, had always been the Cinderella of the Kentish Coastal piers, which in pre-war days received little more than spasmodic visits from the Belle Steamers excursions from London, and [the town] did not cater for the Kent and Essex [excursion] clientele. It was not an easy matter to open up the route, with just the small amount of shipping available; the larger *City of Rochester* was needed for the heavy Strood to Southend traffic, with the *Princess of Wales* in relief, this being a seven-day-a-week service, leaving only the little *Audrey* available, having a capacity of 600 passengers and a speed of just 12 knots. It would be a heavy day's work to maintain the schedule and snags would arise, more often than not when least expected.'

Unsurprisingly, the little steamer was put in the charge of the senior master, Captain Tommy Aldis. For the initial 1923 season the *Audrey* was scheduled to leave Sun Pier at Chatham at 8.00am direct for Southend. The normal Chatham, Strood and Southend boat would not leave until 9.00am, offering a more leisurely day. The *Audrey*, however, would have already left Southend at 10.00am to pick up local passengers at Sheerness en route for Herne Bay, where she arrived for the first time in the day at 12.45pm. She then cruised to Southend and back, leaving Herne Bay again at 3.45pm, and picking up non-landing cruise passengers at Southend for one more trip to Herne Bay.

And here was the snag – so popular were the afternoon cruises to Herne Bay that the ship was often over-capacity for her evening departure from Herne Bay. Unless the *Princess of Wales* was able to help, passengers inevitably had to be left behind – some careful arithmetic by the Southend agent became an essential part of the longer-term company public relations strategy that year! Despite this problem, the season was a great success and Captain Aldis brought his little steamer through all the difficulties of the new route with flying colours.

The operational pressures on the company were released considerably the following season when the brand-new steamer *Medway Queen* was commissioned and a second-hand steamer was brought into the fleet. This was proof positive that Captain Shippick really meant business, and the name of his new steamer heralded a totally new trading banner, 'The Queen Line of Steamers'. Delivered from the Ailsa Shipbuilding Company at Troon, and launched by the wife of the

The *City of Rochester* (1904) seen off Southend Pier following her post-war renovation in which the lounge was plated in to the front of the Promenade Deck.

Chairman of the New Medway Steam Packet Company, Mrs Charles Willis, the *Medway Queen* was distinctive in that the Promenade Deck was continued to the bows but fell short of the rope-handling area aft. She was a handy-sized vessel for the Medway trade at 316 gross tons, and her compound diagonal engines drove her along at a comfortable 15 knots.

The privilege of taking the *Medway Queen* out on her maiden voyage on Friday 18 July 1924 fell to Captain C. Scott. Embarking a civic party at Southend Pier, she made a cruise to Herne Bay, where, it was reported, it was too choppy to land the official party. For the remainder of the season the *Medway Queen* was given to Captain Aldis to look after on the Strood to Southend route.

The second ship to enter the fleet in 1924 was the *Queen of the South*, formerly with Channel Excursion Steamers Limited at Brighton, and in pre-war days none other than the *Woolwich Belle*. She was able to release the *City of Rochester*, which then took over some of the Herne Bay duties from the *Audrey* and began to develop new routes as far afield as Clacton. The *Audrey*, in turn, was trialling new services to Margate and Ramsgate via Herne Bay. These developments left little room for the elderly *Princess of Wales*, which was now rarely in steam and then only in a relief capacity or helping in the height of the season on the Herne Bay and Southend excursions.

In 1925 the *Medway Queen* was able to cut a new furrow. Following in the wake of the *City of Rochester*, she now set about developing the Medway to Southend, Clacton, Felixstowe and Walton route. In December 1925 Captain Shippick added another new steamer to his navy, the *Walton Belle*, which he bought from the East Anglian Steamship Company. In 1926, under the Queen Line of Steamers name *Essex Queen*, this vessel took over the Chatham to Sheerness, Southend and Margate run. The elderly (and slow) *Princess of Wales* was chartered out for service on the Firth of Forth, but she was not a success, later sinking at her moorings. She was scrapped in 1928.

Shippick's determined expansion was based on two premises. One was that the Belle Steamers/Royal Sovereign fleets were in terminal

The *Medway Queen*: a special ship

There have been few ships so dear to their patrons. In her final year of service in 1963, the *Medway Queen* was followed closely by the media, who cried out for her to be preserved. But she was special: at Dunkirk she was special, she was always special coming alongside at Southend, and above all she was my special ship.

Colin Fleetney described a visit to the engine room alleyways in an article in *Paddle Wheels*, May 1971:

> 'I positioned myself at the engine room rail of the port alleyway, a wide well-lighted thoroughfare, which together with that on the starboard side, connects all accommodation below deck. I reached the rail and the brass needle of the telegraph moved to "slow astern". The third engineer moved the repeater, and the Chief the levers on the manoeuvring platform. Crossheads swept up the gleaming guides, paused and returned. Cranks rose and fell. Brass lubricators flashed and winked. Behind me through the ship's side came the rumble of the feathering eccentric as the wheel turned.
>
> Ranged round the engine room, below the side alleys, are the usual auxiliaries associated with the running of a steam ship. Up on the manoeuvring platform are the steering and fan engines, the former never failing to attract attention by its sudden eruptions of power as the Quartermaster cons the ship down the busy river, while the latter throbs at high speed supplying air to the boiler fires. Steam for all the machinery is supplied by one boiler. When the safety valves lift, a singularly rare occurrence, they do so at a pressure of 140 pounds per square inch.'

The *Medway Queen* was quite beamy in proportion to her depth. She had an open bridge forward of the paddles and the funnel and a single mast. Down the main companionway on the Main Deck was a small tea room and ice cream kiosk, and aft of the machinery spaces was the main dining room with the pantry right aft. The dining room spanned the full width of the

The *Medway Queen* (1924) running down the Medway in the 1930s. *George Robins collection*

ship, and was light and airy with sea views through the curtained picture windows. The dining room was served by waitresses who always seemed to remain calm, no matter how full the room became. Emergency oil lights were retained throughout all the public rooms and these swung in their gimbals as the ship pitched in mid-estuary.

Below the dining room was the lounge, with the Acorn Bar forward. The lounge was longer than the bar and had portholes close to the water line. Colin Fleetney continues:

> 'This room, similar to the room above in that it is the full width of the ship, is much larger and more comfortable than its counterpart, the Acorn Bar, forward. The oak and teak panelling, and settees and easy chairs in matching moquette, the tables dotted about in an informal manner, all helped to create a warm club-like atmosphere. As the ship was heeling slightly to port the portholes on that side were just submerged beneath the wake of the paddle wheel, and through them the sea shimmered a light green, scored by millions of air bubbles. From the aft starboard porthole it was just possible to see under the paddle box; as she lifted and rolled a little more to port I caught a brief glimpse of the wheel. For a few seconds floats and arms were silhouetted black against the sea, pounding and tearing at the surface. Then the ship returned to her almost even keel, and the sea leapt at the porthole sending spray whipping at the glass.'

The area between the dining saloon and the tea room was by far the most interesting. There were doors to the sponsons fore and aft, and the upper part of one or other was usually open for ventilation. Here the passenger realised by sight and smell how close the sea was, and here through a porthole into the paddle box could be seen the floats and rods in the dim spray-filled light. There were two alleyways connecting the forward part of the Main Deck with the aft part either side of the engine room. Over polished brass rails the passengers could look down on the flashing rods and thrusting crossheads of the engines and the control platform – a small boy transfixed and oblivious of his dripping ice cream, now a white puddle on the deck! Between the two engine room windows was a rounded steel ridge across the deck polished by the feet of passers by. This was the cover over the paddle shaft.

The warm alleyways on the Main Deck contrasted with the breezes of the Promenade Deck despite the sponson doors always being open. The Boat Deck was uncluttered with only the Purser's Cabin beneath the bridge, and the lifeboats on the after part of each sponson. Buoyant seating and life raft containers were plentiful, and apart from the numerous dark brown ventilators and the engine room skylights, the tall funnel gave some small respite from the breeze and a little warmth.

The *Queen of the South* (1891) joined Captain Shippick's navy in 1924. She was the former *Woolwich Belle* and was eventually sold for scrap in 1932 for £300.

The New Medway Steam Packet Company's *Essex Queen* (1897), formerly the *Walton Belle*, before alterations (*above*) and minus funnel cowl but with the forward lounge extended to the full width of the ship (*below*).

decline through mismanagement and lack of capital. The other was that the motor coach and the railway train were there to bring steamer passengers from London to Southend, where they could then embark on a sea trip. What joy was there to be had in sailing down a dirty and congested river from Greenwich to Southend? Besides, those who chose to do so were adequately catered for by the daily sailings of GSN's *Eagle* and *Golden Eagle*. Fresh Wharf had, in any case, not been made available to the steamers after the war until 1925. Little by little 'Captain Shippick's navy' was beginning to dominate the excursion trade.

GSN recognised the threat and realised that its *Eagle* was no longer ideal for attracting the London down-river trade. This, then, was the background to the company placing an order with J. Samuel White & Company at Cowes for a large, fast and prestigious steamer. The outcome was the *Crested Eagle*, a magnificent paddle steamer of 1,100 tons

Above The *Eagle* (1898), now with only one mast.

Below The *Golden Eagle* (1906) in post-war guise with white ventilators.

The *Crested Eagle* (1925) was the first pleasure steamer to be built with oil-burning furnaces. *George Robins collection*

THE
ROYAL THAMES

"CRESTED EAGLE"
ONE-DAY LUXURY CRUISES
FROM THE HEART OF LONDON
*Daily (except Fridays), leaving
TOWER OF LONDON PIER .. 9.20 a.m.
GREENWICH PIER .. .. .. 9.50 "
NORTH WOOLWICH PIER .. 10.15 "
(Weather and other circumstances permitting)

SOUTHEND and CLACTON

FARES	SINGLE	DAY RETURN Mon., Tues., Wed., Thurs.	DAY RETURN Sats.	DAY RETURN Sundays	PERIOD RETURN
SOUTHEND	3/-	4/-	5/-	5/-	5/-
CLACTON	5/6	6/-	6/-	8/-	9/-

CHILDREN UNDER 14 HALF-PRICE
All Bank Holiday Day-Return Fares at Saturday Day-Return Fares.
Passengers are carried only on the terms and conditions printed on the Company's Tickets.
The General Steam Navigation Co., Ltd., 15, Trinity Square, London, E.C.3.
Telephone: Royal 3200. Ext. 8.
Book to
MARK LANE
for
Tower Pier

gross that was launched on 25 March 1925 and placed on the Fresh Wharf to Ramsgate service, with the *Eagle* and *Golden Eagle* still based at Greenwich. Frank Burtt described the *Crested Eagle* as follows:

> 'Like the *Golden Eagle*, the commodious Promenade Deck of this steamer ran from the bow to within a few feet of the stern post, the hull being divided into ten compartments by watertight bulkheads. The foremast was hinged and the funnel made telescopic for the purpose of passing under London Bridge to take up her station at the Old Swan Pier. A bow rudder assisted the steering when going astern. As in the *Golden Eagle*, the motive power was obtained from triple-expansion engines, which could give a speed of over 18 knots. The *Crested Eagle* was the first Thames pleasure steamer to be fitted for burning oil fuel.'

As built, she had a three-barrel concertina-type funnel, each barrel narrower than the one below it. This was found to be a problematical arrangement and the vessel was returned to her builders after the first season to re-emerge with a twin-barrel funnel, the bottom fixed section being, therefore, somewhat taller than that of the former triple-barrel arrangement. The top section was seldom fully raised, however, giving the vessel the characteristic stumpy funnel appearance for which she is remembered to this day.

The *Crested Eagle* was a hugely popular vessel and quickly became known as the 'Greyhound of the River'. She had a service speed of 18.5 knots and could accommodate 1,650 passengers. However, she entered a world where wages were depressed and disposable incomes were declining.

The prudence of her owners opting for oil-burning boilers was very quickly demonstrated, for in 1926 the General Strike voiced a brief cry of desperation from the hard-pressed workers, while the coal miners opted to stay out on strike. This placed non-essential traffic such as coal-burning excursion steamers a long way down the priority list, and many ships were laid up for at least part of the season.

Despite the harsh trading conditions, Captain Shippick was determined to get into the continental no-passport day trip traffic. However, the fleet he now had at his disposal was barely sufficient to service his Margate and Ramsgate and his Clacton, Felixstowe and Walton routes, together with the Southend and Herne Bay commitments. Watchful for useful second-hand tonnage, Shippick turned to the Admiralty. Since the war all the surviving *Ascot* class paddle minesweepers had been swinging round their anchor chains growing barnacles. Although many of them had been sold for scrap in 1922, five were kept in waiting and put on the market only in 1927. Captain Shippick had the vessels inspected and offered to buy HMS *Atherstone*, a product of the Ailsa Shipbuilding Company at Troon. The other four were duly dispatched to breakers' yards.

The *Atherstone* was stripped internally and reconstructed as a pleasure steamer in the true style of the biblical prophesy 'beating swords into plough shares'. Although she would be slower than her new fleet-mates, at only 16 knots, she would allow Captain Shippick to move into the continental trade. The conversion at the company's own Acorn yard complete, the new excursion steamer, renamed *Queen of Kent*, entered service in June 1928. Only her silhouette remained broadly the same, with the widely spaced funnels and prominent bridge structure behind the mainmast, and the distinctive cruiser stern characteristic of the *Ascot* class. Gone were the lookout turrets, the mine wire derricks and the boom that once hung over the stern. Here was a neat day passenger steamer equipped for excursionists bent on enjoying a day out on the Thames, during which they could forget the hardships of the late 1920s.

While the other *Ascot* class minesweepers had by then been cut up, HMS *Melton* alone was still lying at the yard of Hughes, Bolckow & Company at Blyth. Captain Shippick, so pleased was he with his first purchase, made an offer for the vessel and she was soon steamed round to the Acorn yard. This minesweeper had been built at Port Glasgow by W. Hamilton & Company, but she was destined for the same treatment as the *Atherstone*. She emerged from the Acorn yard with the Queen Line of Steamers name *Queen of Thanet*, ready for the 1929 season. Thus, at relatively little cost, the

The *Queen of Kent* (1916), formerly HMS *Atherstone*, seen in the Thames.

The *Queen of Thanet* (1916), formerly HMS *Melton*, looking resplendent in civilian dress.

Table 5: The New Medway Steam Packet Company's 'Queen Line of Steamers' fleet in 1929

Name	Built	Tons gross	Length (ft)	Speed (knots)	Comments
Queen of Southend	1889	522	240	16[1]	Ex-*Yarmouth Belle*, bought from East Anglia Steamship Company, 1928
Queen of the South	1891	298	200	15	Ex-*Woolwich Belle* 1922, bought from Channel Excursion Steamers, Brighton, 1924
Audrey	1897	203	126	12	Acquired 1922 (formerly owned by Capt Shippick); sold for scrap September 1929
Essex Queen	1897	465	230	16[1]	Ex-*Walton Belle*, bought from East Anglia Steamship Company, December 1925
City of Rochester	1904	235	160	15	Built at J. Scott & Co at Kinghorn, Fife
Queen of Kent	1916	798	235	16	Ex-HMS *Atherstone*, bought from Admiralty, 1927, and refitted at Rochester
Queen of Thanet	1916	792	235	16	Ex-HMS *Melton*, bought from shipbreakers, 1928, and refitted at Rochester
Medway Queen	1924	318	180	15	Built at Ailsa Shipbuilding Co, Troon

[1] Formerly capable of 17 knots (when built)

Above The *Queen of Southend* (1889), formerly the *Yarmouth Belle*, seen before the 1936 season, when she had the forward saloon replaced by a new saloon plated to the bow with Promenade Deck to match.

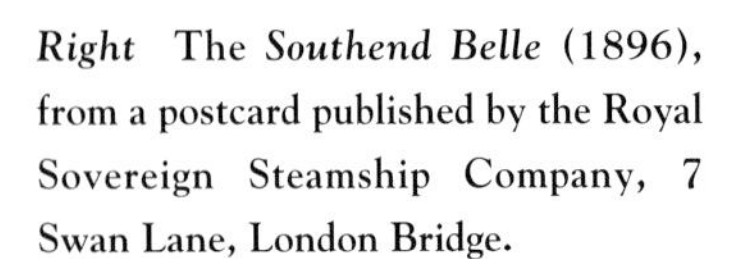

Right The *Southend Belle* (1896), from a postcard published by the Royal Sovereign Steamship Company, 7 Swan Lane, London Bridge.

Left East Anglian Hotels' *Laguna Belle* (1896), the former *Southend Belle*, with a blue band on the funnel and distinctive chevron at the bow.

company added two stalwarts to its fleet. After trials on the Southend and Herne Bay routes, the two sisters were put in charge of the new routes, which included trips to Calais, Boulogne, Dunkirk or Dover from Gravesend, with calls at Margate, or from Sheerness and Southend to Clacton and on to Yarmouth, both returning the same day.

One more addition to the fleet was made in 1929. This was the *Yarmouth Belle*, made available when the East Anglian Steamship Company and RS Steamship Company both ceased trading against mounting debts. Previously, at the end of the 1928 season, both the *London Belle* and the *Clacton Belle*, reputedly heavy coal-burners, had been sold for scrapping. Early in 1929 the *Yarmouth Belle* adopted the Queen Line name *Queen of Southend*, while the *Southend Belle* was 'sold' to Mr Kingsman and East Anglia Hotels Limited to become the *Laguna Belle*, and the good old *Royal Sovereign* went to GSN, the latter perhaps fearful that the New Medway Steam Packet was beginning to take control. Indeed, Captain Shippick now had the dominant fleet on the Thames, and while GSN had the biggest and the newest steamers, the New Medway Steam Packet Company was very much in charge.

The demise of Belle Steamers was partly because of an unwillingness to adapt its trading patterns to changing demands. An article in *Sea Breezes* in June 1962 reported:

> 'Sailings [had] continued on the old Belle routes, and in the 1924 season the *Walton Belle* was based at Harwich and advertised to leave on Sundays, Tuesdays and Thursdays for Felixstowe, Walton, Clacton and Margate, allowing passengers an hour and half there before she returned by the same route. On Wednesdays she left Harwich at 8.00am for Clacton, Walton, Felixstowe, Southwold and Lowestoft, taking 5 hours and 45 minutes each way and allowing passengers 2 hours in the terminal port while she made a sea cruise.
>
> Under the East Anglian Steamship Company, in the 1926 season a "Belle" sailed daily from London (Friday excepted) for Southend, Clacton and Walton, with additional calls at Felixstowe, Southwold, Lowestoft and Yarmouth in the mid-season. London to Yarmouth sailing time was about 11 hours in good weather and the return was made the following day to Greenwich or Woolwich. London sailings at this period started from Old Swan Pier where tenders embarked 200 to 300 passengers at a time for the "Belle" moorings in the Pool.'

Belle Steamers was no more, the 'Belles' dispersed to other owners or dispatched to the scrapyards. But the hard times of the 1920s were set to get worse. To add insult to injury, of the two former 'Belle' steamers, the *Queen of Southend* usually ran from Chatham to Felixstowe while the *Queen of the South* was placed at Yarmouth to provide the daily connection to Felixstowe. The latter was abandoned in 1930 and replaced by a coach service.

During the 1929 season, Captain Shippick's all-time favourite, the little steamer *Audrey*, spent the summer operating short coastal cruises from Ramsgate. Now totally outclassed by her fleet-mates, she was dispatched in September to Thomas Ward in return for a scrap price of just £500.

Meanwhile, GSN welcomed the *Royal Sovereign* into its fleet and sent the *Eagle* straight off to the breakers, as she had been dogged with mechanical problems in her old age. The *Royal Sovereign* appeared on the Margate run in 1929 altered only by the addition of a thin black top to her funnel. She was clearly a 'make do' purchase and, had trading conditions been more favourable, a new build would almost certainly have been ordered as replacement for the *Eagle*. As it was, the *Royal Sovereign* was herself put up for sale at the end of the 1929 season, and purchased for £3,500 by Dutch shipbreakers.

During the winter the *Golden Eagle* was converted to oil fuel. W. G. Peake describes this in his role as Chief Engineer in an article that first appeared in *Paddle Wheels*, Summer 1975:

> 'In the winter of 1929/1930, it was decided to convert the ship to oil burning and I had to stand by in the winter to carry this out. It turned out to be a very interesting job; the existing coal bunkers had to be cut away, new oil tanks made and fitted. The fuel burning

The *Royal Sovereign* (1893) approaching one of the Thames piers.

installation had to be fitted, and all the pipelines installed. I must say that in 1930 when we were bunkered with oil for the first time on this ship, and then lit the fires, it was a great success.

We found it wasn't all rosy. The procedure for oiling in London was that the first ship back at night was first to get the oiling barge, and as we got back late, our time for bunkering came about 2.00 in the morning and, of course, two engineers had to attend to this. Fortunately we only took bunkers every other night.'

As the 1920s closed, Britain found itself in the grip of the Great Depression. Ship owners were beginning to suffer as business diminished and competition intensified, particularly on the Atlantic trades. Captain Shippick's navy needed to stay on top of the Thames excursion business if it was going to keep GSN in its place.

9. DEPRESSION – WHAT DEPRESSION?

'Even as the open-top omnibus was replaced by one with a covered top deck, so the excursion steamer became an all-weather craft by being provided with spacious deck shelters where the passengers could sit in comfortable easy chairs without being either blown to pieces or drenched to the skin. The prototype of this class was the *Royal Eagle*, built in 1932, the largest paddle steamer in the country; she was 1,538 gross tons and, with a speed of 18 knots, was half a knot or so slower than her very popular sister *Crested Eagle*...'

G. W. Tripp, *Sea Breezes*, July 1949

In the depths of the Depression, the Blue Star Line resorted to running its fabulous luxury cruise ship *Arandora Star* on day trips from Bournemouth at £1 per head. Cunard's *Berengaria*, dubbed the 'Bargain Area', was meanwhile operating short-duration cheap cruises out of New York, to be enjoyed by all. The 1930s were hard times for all the ship owners. However, on the Thames the pleasure steamers carried on business as normal, Londoners content to spend what disposable cash they had on a day out by the sea.

For the 1930 season only, an intruder could be seen at Southend. The Angleterre-Lorraine-Alsace Société Anonyme de Navigation had the French cross-Channel steam ferry *Lorrain* spare. Built as the *Rathmore* for the Holyhead to Greenore route in 1908, she was transferred in 1927, together with three other vessels from the former London & North Western Railway, to operate a new route for the French company between Tilbury and Dunkirk. In the summer months of 1930 she was rostered to leave Southend at 8.00am, or 9.00am on Saturdays, Sundays and Mondays, with a return from Dunkirk at 6.00pm. The *Lorrain* was a big ship to fill and was not entirely successful on the Southend service. She was withdrawn and scrapped three years later when the UK ferry terminal was switched from Tilbury to Folkestone.

Meanwhile, the *Laguna Belle*, formally Belle Steamers' *Southend Belle* and now operated by East Anglian Hotels, had become an immediate success. East Anglian Hotels was set on maintaining pier tolls and visitor numbers to Clacton and this it achieved with cheap fares of only 4 shillings for a day trip from the new Tower Pier to Clacton. She was given attractive funnel colours of yellow with a blue band and carried a snazzy, almost art deco, blue-and-white-edged 'bite' painted on her bows, and, horror of horrors, she was given one of the first, if not the first, floating amusement saloons. After her first season with her new owner she was sent back to her builder, William Denny at Dumbarton, to be reboilered, although still coal-fired, and to have the fore lounge extended to the sides of the ship. Calling at Greenwich and Woolwich only, the *Laguna Belle* averaged more than 900 passengers per trip and usually ran to capacity at weekends.

As Tannoy systems were introduced to the vessels, the traditional live band was slowly replaced by the gramophone. Naturally, each ship adopted its own signature tune and, logically, each time the *Laguna Belle* approached one of its piers strains of 'Lily of Laguna' would be heard across the water. The *Royal Eagle*, which was to be commissioned for the 1932 season, had an unfortunate habit of playing 'Open Up Dem Pearly Gates' each time she approached Tower Bridge, and of course 'La Marseillaise' was obligatory for any steamer entering a French port.

In 1930 the Port of London Authority inaugurated schools cruises round the dock system using a series of small motor boats. The cruises were very popular and a contract was let to the New Medway Steam Packet Company for the 1931 and 1932 seasons to operate the cruises. This was a Wednesday duty normally operated by the *Essex Queen*; it required her to pick up at Southend and London for the cruise, after starting at Chatham in the late morning, and returning in the late evening. Use of the larger steamers allowed the cruises to be opened to the general public.

The company had converted a number of steamers to oil-burning the previous winter. Both the *Essex Queen* and *Queen of Southend* were converted at Rochester, and their accommodation upgraded, and the *Queen of Thanet* and *Queen of Kent* were similarly dealt with; the latter pair were also given new paddle wheels, which gave them a slight increase in speed. The 1931 season was the last for the *Queen of the South*, the former *Woolwich Belle*, now 40 years old, and she was sold for scrap during 1932 for a paltry £300.

The year 1932, however, was a special one on the Thames. GSN demonstrated its confidence in the recovery of the nation's economy by commissioning the magnificent and luxuriously appointed paddle steamer *Royal Eagle*. The New Medway Steam Packet Company invaded GSN territory by running a direct steamer service daily from London, usually with *Queen of Southend*. The

THE
ROYAL THAMES

The "ROYAL EAGLE"

ONE-DAY LUXURY CRUISES
FROM THE HEART OF LONDON
(Weather and other circumstances permitting)
*Daily (except Fridays) from
TOWER OF LONDON PIER .. 9.0 a.m.
GREENWICH PIER .. .. 9.30 "
NORTH WOOLWICH PIER .. 10.0 "

TO	FARES SINGLE.	DAY RETURN. Mon., Tues., Wed., Thurs.	PERIOD RETURN or DAY RETURN. Sats. and Suns. and Bank Holidays.
SOUTHEND -	3/-	4/-	5/-
MARGATE -	6/-	8/-	10/-
RAMSGATE -	6/6	9/-	11/-

All Bank Holiday Day-Return Fares at Saturday Day-Return Fares.
CHILDREN UNDER 14 HALF-PRICE.
A supplementary charge of 1/- per single journey (1/6 return) for use of the Sun Deck, payable on board, including use of deck chairs available.
Passengers are carried only on the terms and conditions printed on the Company's Tickets.
Excellent Breakfasts, Luncheons and Teas. Fully Licensed.
The General Steam Navigation Co., Ltd., 15, Trinity Square, London, E.C.3.
Telephone: Royal 2200. Ext. 8.
Book to MARK LANE for Tower Pier

'Open Up Dem Pearly Gates' with the *Royal Eagle* (1932).

Above An aerial view of the *Royal Eagle* (1932) showing her expansive and uncluttered decks.

Above right and right Part of the Main Dining Saloon aboard the *Royal Eagle* (*above*) and the ship's 'Old Time' Smoking Room.

The Southern Railway steamer *Engadine* (1911) ran from Tower Pier to the Nore Light during the 1932 season with an all-yellow funnel. She is seen waiting at the buoys in the Pool of London for her passengers to arrive by tender.

screw steamer *Rochester Queen*, a replacement for the *Queen of the South*, entered service on the Rochester to Southend route; she was the former Tilbury to Gravesend ferry *Gertrude*, dating from 1906. The *Gertrude* had become surplus to requirements when the Tilbury Passenger Terminal and deep-water landing stage became available in 1930, greatly reducing the demand for the ferries to act also as passenger tenders to liners anchored off Gravesend.

Another interloper from the railway companies appeared with the charter of the Southern Railway turbine ferry *Engadine* by S. Instone & Company for cruises from Tower Pier to a point 20 miles beyond the Nore Light, leaving at 10.45am and returning at 5.00pm without any calls en route. The charter lasted for the months of June, July and August, but the *Engadine* was not well patronised and the experiment was not repeated in subsequent years.

Also in 1932 a new concept was introduced with the elderly South Coast paddle steamer *Alexandra*, which initiated a floating show and dance venue under the banner 'The Showboat'. She had been bought from Cosens & Company by a Captain Hawkes and Mr Whitley, who intended to provide a Mississippi-style showboat cabaret, and she was based at Westminster Pier. She either ran up-river towards Richmond, using her newly hinged mast and funnel, or down to Greenwich, but her extensive new ornate deckhouse, containing the cabaret area, so increased her airdraft that passage upstream was only possible at very specific stages of the tide. The following year, with boilers now cold, the *Alexandra* spent much of August wallowing at anchor off Margate. After the show had finished, revellers invariably departed for the pier on the tender, suffering the effects of mal de mer. The *Alexandra* was then moved to Shoreham Harbour, where she was modified for use on the Manchester Ship Canal, but as cash ran out work stopped and she was returned to the Thames in November 1934 and demolished.

The *Royal Eagle* was the last of all the Thames paddlers to be built, and the first to have observation lounges and a Sun Deck, and the first and only Thames steamer to be built by Cammell Laird at Birkenhead. Although the bridge remained abaft the funnel in order to assist conning the ship astern in confined waters, notably through Tower Bridge into the congested waters of the Pool, she was otherwise innovative in that she had forced-draught oil-fired Scotch boilers feeding triple-expansion engines. She was also distinctive in that she had two masts. Her built-up appearance gave an impression of size, and although she was 10 feet shorter in length than the *Crested Eagle*, she was larger at 1,539 gross tons. The *Royal Eagle*, with accommodation for 2,000 passengers on four decks, was the most luxurious vessel yet. Her lounges and other public rooms were fitted out to a very high standard, and the dining rooms, which could seat 300, were second to none, being serviced by a catering staff of 70. She took up service on the Tower Pier to Southend, Margate and Ramsgate route, for which she had been designed, and on which route she stayed throughout the remainder of the decade. The displaced *Crested Eagle* then moved to a new Tower Pier for Southend, Clacton and Felixstowe service in direct competition with the *Laguna Belle*.

Apparently there was considerable investigation of motive power before the design of the *Royal Eagle* was finalised. Consideration of screw propulsion and direct-drive diesel engines was in the end given up in favour of steam and paddles. This decision hinged on the confined seaways the ship used, often requiring her to go astern up the river after dark to Tower Pier, and the known ability of the paddle steamer to cope with the difficult conditions at the exposed pier head berths in the estuary. The direct-drive diesel and the diesel-electric drive were then already in use in the ferry fleets of David MacBrayne and the Southampton, Isle of Wight & South of England Company, and were being championed by the Danish ferry company DFDS and the Coast Lines Group of companies, which had introduced the *Ulster Monarch* and her many sisters from 1929 onwards.

Eagle Steamers' marketing included descriptive titles for each ship, which reflected their on-board character. The *Royal Eagle* was 'London's Own Luxury Liner', the *Crested Eagle* was the 'Greyhound of the River' and the *Golden Eagle* was always 'The Happy Ship'. It was not uncommon for King Neptune to hold his Court on the afterdeck of the *Golden Eagle*. The contemporary Eagle Steamers Handbook takes up the theme:

> 'We lay claim that once you are aboard the *Golden Eagle* there is not a dull moment. Sports and games start immediately on leaving the pier, the kiddies find real fun and enjoyment in the balloon blowing competitions, skipping, musical chairs, tug-of-war and streamer throwing. Even the grown-ups cannot be kept out; they become young once again, and want to enter into the fun with all the keenness of the youngsters. Soon all are one great big family – hence our slogan "The Happy Ship".'

Competition on the London to Clacton route was intense in 1932, with the *Crested Eagle* and *Laguna Belle* running down from Tower Pier and the *Queen of Southend* from Greenwich, but all vying for the same trade. The New Medway Steam Packet Company's Queen Line 'upped the ante' the following year by basing both the *Queen of Southend* and the *Essex Queen* at Fresh Wharf, just below London Bridge. The *Queen of Southend* ran a day-return circuit to Felixstowe via Greenwich, Woolwich, Southend and Clacton, and the *Essex Queen* really trod on GSN's toes by running daily to Southend, Herne Bay, Margate and Ramsgate. There was often considerable confusion as to which ship was on which roster at Fresh Wharf as they were boarded with one vessel alongside the other in the morning.

The *Crested Eagle* ran on the Clacton route for part of the 1933 season, but was not a success. W. G. Peake takes up the story again:

> 'I duly took over the *Crested Eagle* [as Chief Engineer] and promptly was put on the London, Southend, Clacton, Walton and Felixstowe service. This did not last long, about six weeks I think, as we were arriving back in London too late at night and passengers were complaining. This requires a little explanation, for the schedule was timed properly according to her speed and on paper could do the time easily. The snag was the shallow water over the Wallet to Clacton and between Clacton and Felixstowe. It did not matter how fast the ship was: only a very limited speed could be obtained over the shallows and we found we had to slow down accordingly. At nearly low water over the Wallet the vessel's bottom would almost touch at slow speed and then the trouble would commence.

Some of the first motor excursion ships

Development of the marine internal combustion engine was such that by the early 1930s a number of cross-Channel and deep-sea ships had successfully demonstrated both the viability and economics of the new engine. The Danish ferry company DFDS, for example, had the 16-knot *Parkeston* and *Jylland* in service powered by six-cylinder Burmeister & Wain diesels in 1925 and 1926 respectively. Then the Coast Line group of companies had the 17- and 18-knot *Ulster Monarch* and her numerous brothers and sisters in operation on the overnight Irish Sea services from 1929 onwards. The very first fast day passenger ferry was the Belgian *Prince Baudouin*, designed for the 22½-knot Dover to Ostend service and commissioned in 1934 – she actually attained 25 knots on trials. Coincidentally the *Prince Baudouin* came under the management of GSN on behalf of the Ministry of War Transport for a period during the Second World War.

It was logical that the excursion operators should look to the diesel as the successor to the paddle wheel and the steam reciprocating engine. There were three different classes of pioneer motor ship built for the excursion trade:

- the part-time ferry, part-time excursion ship;
- the smaller and slower ships built for local cruising; and
- the innovative, large and fast ships built for the New Medway Steam Packet Company and the General Steam Navigation Company for cross-Channel excursion traffic.

It is the third of these, the *Queen of the Channel*-type vessel, that was pivotal to the development and promotion of the diesel engine for fast day passenger ferries. Uptake was slow because the railway fleets were content with coal and steam in their relatively non-competitive environment, while other excursion operators had already invested heavily in conventional technology and could not yet adopt the diesel engine.

One of the pioneer operators of motor-driven passenger ships was the Scottish ferry operator David MacBrayne Limited. The mother of all the internal-combustion-engined passenger ferries was the triple-screw motor vessel *Lochinvar*, which was completed in 1908 and equipped with three six-cylinder paraffin engines. She was ordered with the experience of two earlier paraffin 'steamers', one of which was later destroyed when her engines exploded. Although never employed as an excursion ship in Scotland, the *Lochinvar* came south and sported the name *Anzio I* in her old age, when she maintained excursions between Southend and Sheerness for the Thames & Medway Navigation Company between 1961 and 1963 (see Chapter 11).

David MacBrayne's twin-funnel diesel-electric *Lochfyne* was the ultimate part-time ferry, part-time excursion motor ship. She was built by William Denny in 1931 with Davey Paxman diesels and Metro-Vickers electric motors coupled to twin screws, a system that overcame the engine manoeuvres required of the direct-drive engine; she could maintain more than 16 knots but suffered serious vibration problems throughout her life. She had accommodation for 1,200 passengers, there being no cargo space, and a gross tonnage of 748 tons. She operated excursions based on Oban and Fort William, but in later years is well remembered for her service on the Clyde to Tarbert and Ardrishaig. She was withdrawn from service in 1969, and eventually broken up in 1974.

Typical of the small type of ships built for local cruising were the Scarborough ships of the 1930s. The first motor ship at Scarborough was the *Royal Lady*, which was built in 1934 by John Crown & Sons at Sunderland for local owners Thomas Round & Sons. Her gross tonnage was a mere 195, but she had two squat funnels, giving her the appearance of a mini-liner, a full-length Promenade Deck and comfortable accommodation for 475 passengers for the standard 2-hour cruise up the coast. She was replaced in 1938 by the bigger and faster *New Royal Lady*, which had only two seasons at Scarborough before the war, and thereafter resumed commercial work by operating for new owners out of Kirkcaldy in 1947 under the name *Royal Lady*. She was renamed the *Crested Eagle* on sale to GSN in 1951. She initially maintained the London Docks cruises, but in 1952 and 1953 was stationed at Ramsgate for local cruises. Thereafter she was put on the Gravesend to Southend and Clacton route (see Chapter 11).

The present-day *Coronia* is also a 1930s diesel excursion ship, smaller and less imposing, but nevertheless dedicated to the excursion trade since her birth at Great Yarmouth in 1935. She was built by Fellows & Company as the *Brit* for the local firm of Longfield Brothers, for whom she operated excursions to Scroby Sands. In the immediate post-war years she served the Festival of Britain as part of the Thames Launches fleet with a passenger capacity of 136, then went to Scarborough in 1951 as Dalton & Round's *Yorkshire Lady*.

One of the pioneer diesel passenger ships on the Thames was the *New Dagenham*, built in Holland in 1933 for the Odelia Cruising Motor Ship Company, a subsidiary of R. G. Odell, which operated lighterage services on the river. The *New Dagenham* had twin engines and a gross tonnage of 255. She operated mainly between Westminster and the Ford works at Dagenham, but undertook special public cruises every Sundays. She was sold in 1937.

The biggest investment in diesel excursion ships was made by the New Medway Steam Packet Company in conjunction with William Denny of Dumbarton in 1935, when the innovative cross-Channel excursion ship *Queen of the Channel* was put into service. Much of Denny's earlier experience in building the *Lochfyne* and her near sister *Lochnevis* was instrumental in the success of the design and construction of the *Queen of the Channel*. She was the first of the big motor excursion ships aimed at the cross-Channel traffic and the commitment made to her by Captain Shippick and the team at Denny underlines the faith that both parties had in the proposed design and motive power.

The importance of the *Queen of the Channel* in the development of the faster cross-Channel excursion ship and fast cross-Channel passenger ferry cannot be overstated. Her success can be judged by the subsequent orders for two larger and faster vessels, the *Royal Sovereign* and *Royal Daffodil*, and subsequently by a further two ships to replace war losses. She was also instrumental in Denny successfully taking the idea of a motor ferry to the London, Midland & Scottish Railway, which received the first large diesel railway ferry, the equally innovative stern-loading car ferry *Princess Victoria*, in 1939. (Her post-war replacement of the same name was lost under tragic circumstances in a storm in 1953.)

The vacuum would go back from 25 inches to 10 inches and we knew we had a job to do that night. The main injectors would take in vast quantities of seaweed and mussels and these would get across the tubes in the main condenser like a mat and no amount of blowing steam would move it. It meant that on arrival at the buoys at night after a slow passage home we would have to remove the condenser doors, clear all the stoppages and box up again. When all these considerations were weighed up it was decided to abandon Felixstowe and stop at Clacton and do a sea trip.'

The continental routes were maintained again by the *Queen of Thanet* and *Queen of Kent*, one from Clacton and one from Gravesend. However, the Port of London Authority contract for the docks cruises was lost to rivals GSN, although it did not at first have a vessel available. Again sights were set on redundant tonnage from the Clyde, and the 41-year-old steamer *Isle of Arran* was purchased from the Williamson Buchanan fleet, her place on the Clyde being taken by the new turbine steamer *Queen Mary* (which today lies on the Thames alongside the Embankment opposite the Queen Elizabeth Hall). The *Isle of Arran* finished on the Clyde on the Spring Bank Holiday weekend and

The *Isle of Arran* (1892) in GSN livery on the Thames.

entered service on the Thames a few days later, resplendent with a red funnel and black top and with a grey hull. Just why she was given these unique colours is not apparent, but it was a refreshing change from the black hulls and yellow funnels with thin black tops of the rest of the GSN excursion fleet, if only for her first year of service on the Thames. For the first time for many years, a simple diagonal engine powered by a 'haystack' boiler was back at work on the Thames. Adorned in the conventional company livery for the 1934 season, the *Isle of Arran* was sold for scrap in October 1936.

The 'new' *Isle of Arran* was put to work on the docks cruises on Wednesdays and Saturdays and otherwise employed on relief services to Herne Bay and Margate or trips to the Nore Light and back. Occasionally, if bookings on the docks cruises were heavy, one of the Tilbury to Gravesend ferries would be chartered to support the *Isle of Arran* for the day.

At the end of the 1933 season the New Medway Steam Packet Company disposed of the *Rochester Queen* as being too small and too slow for the Rochester and Southend service, and made two purchases. The first was the famously named Wallasey ferry boat *Royal Daffodil*. Captain Shippick had worked with the *Royal Daffodil* in the Great War, and it was known that he had a soft spot for the vessel. He wrote of his involvement with her in a letter to *Sea Breezes* in February 1958, from his retirement home in Jersey:

> 'I served in the Royal Naval reserve attached to and assistant to Flag Captain C-in-C the Nore Minesweeping Section Paddle Steamers. During my period of service I received instructions to report to the Admiralty. On arrival I was met and taken to senior naval officers' quarters, where I was interviewed and given a dispatch box to be delivered to the C-in-C The Nore, Admiralty House, Chatham, or his secretary, but to no one else. On arrival by Admiralty car I carried out my instructions and was given another dispatch box and taken to a paddle minesweeper with steam up. The box contained sailing instructions for the Zeebrugge raid.
>
> Several hundred marines on board HM ships were transferred to the *Daffodil* and *Iris*, constituting the landing party for the mole at Zeebrugge. That night on board HMS *Vindictive* I spoke to an officer, whom I learned later was connected with a leading fireworks firm. He was in charge of the smoke screen to cover the ships and the landing party, but was killed by a German shell. After the ships had sailed we returned to Sheerness.'

The final departure of the *Royal Daffodil* from Merseyside had caused concern lest her name be changed to fit in with the Queen Line nomenclature, and assurances were given by Captain Shippick that, 'You may rest assured the name *Royal Daffodil* will not be altered – on the contrary, we shall treasure it and the ship.' Like the *Rochester Queen*, the *Royal Daffodil* was a screw steamer.

The second purchase made by Captain Shippick was the Southern Railway Isle of Wight ferry *Duchess of Kent*, which was give the name *Clacton Queen*. This paddle steamer had been built in 1897 for the joint service of the London, Brighton & South Coast and the London & South Western railways based at Portsmouth.

For the 1934 season the *Royal Daffodil* replaced the *Rochester Queen* on the Rochester to Southend route, and the *Clacton Queen* was deployed on the Ipswich to Clacton service, while the *City of Rochester* became spare ship at Rochester. Otherwise the business of the fleet continued as before, with GSN and East Anglian Hotels operating largely unchanged schedules.

Burtt described the Thames baptism of the *Clacton Queen*, when, on 10 August in her first season on the Thames, she set out from Clacton for a trip to Chatham with 800 passengers aboard:

> 'On the return journey she had to face a rough sea for 10 hours. When she arrived off Clacton at 10.00pm the sea was so rough that the Captain thought it prudent to stand out to sea rather than try to disembark his passengers at the pier head. At 1.30am the next morning the *Clacton Queen* still had not arrived, although her lights could be seen from the shore, so the lifeboat put out and stood by for some time. Later, as the gale

The *Royal Daffodil* (1906) in the Medway in full New Medway Steam Packet Colours.

The *Clacton Queen* (1897) laid up at Rochester in 1935 before her sale to the Mersey & Blackpool Steamship Company.

subsided, an attempt to land the passengers proved successful.'

The *Clacton Queen* was retained for only two seasons and was sold in 1935 for an excursion service between Blackpool and Liverpool as the *Jubilee Queen*. This was not well supported and the vessel was scrapped in 1939.

In the back rooms of the Acorn Shipyard at Rochester, however, plans were being prepared for a new ship for the continental services. Negotiations with William Denny's shipyard at Dumbarton led to a design that was a development of the 1933-built Clyde turbine steamer *Queen Mary*, but the new excursion ship would be driven by direct-drive diesel coupling.

The new motor ship was named the *Queen of the Channel* at her launch on 3 May 1935, and was delivered on 7 June. She was initially registered under the ownership of a new company, the London & Southend Continental Shipping Company, in which the New Medway Steam Packet Company and William Denny both had extensive financial interests; the ship was delivered at a cost of £68,700. In the event, all Denny's shares had been bought out by the New Medway Steam Packet Company after the first year and the holding company was dissolved. The *Queen of the Channel* was based at Gravesend, and started her day by crossing to Tilbury to pick up railway passengers from Fenchurch Street, then to Southend and Margate before crossing either to Boulogne, Calais or Ostend. For this she required a service speed of 19 knots, although she was normally good for 20 knots.

She was a smart ship, painted white overall with green boot topping and with buff funnels – two of them, as was customary in the 1930s when the mini-liner look was in vogue. The forward funnel was a dummy and was used to store the deck chairs. The engines were Sulzer trunk piston engines, one built by Sulzer in Switzerland and the other built under licence by Denny. Manoeuvring required the engines to be stopped and the reverse crank turned over before compressed air could be injected into the engines to start them in reverse. There was always the fear that an engine would not fire and the ship left to drift, a fear that was compounded by the fierce tidal runs off some of the Thames piers. Care had been taken in her design to fit a large enough compressor to sustain pressure in overlarge air bottles to allow a greater number of manoeuvres than would normally be anticipated without recharging the bottles.

The Promenade Deck was almost fully enclosed, but the Boat Deck was available to passengers who preferred the open decks. The *Queen of the Channel* could accommodate up to 1,414 passengers and offered a comfortable observation lounge forward on the Promenade Deck with large glass windows, as well as the obligatory silver service dining room, lounge and bar on the Main Deck.

Also in 1935, the *Laguna Belle* was purchased by GSN, which retained her on the Tower Pier to Clacton run. The New Medway Steam Packet Company's London base moved from Fresh Wharf to Tower Pier, from where it now competed head to head with GSN.

Yet another obsolescent paddler was bought

The *Queen of the Channel* (1935) in the Medway.

from the Clyde (this time from the shipbreakers) when the Redcliffe Shipping Company of Hull put the *Marchioness of Breadalbane* on short cruises out of Great Yarmouth and Lowestoft to Cromer and Felixstowe. The *Marchioness of Breadalbane* had been built, together with her sister the *Marchioness of Bute*, in 1890 to maintain the Caledonian Steam Packet Company's Wemyss Bay to Bute service after Captain Alexander Campbell had withdrawn his steamers from the route at the end of April 1890. On arrival at Lowestoft and Great Yarmouth, the old steamer struggled to pay her way, but she survived the 1935 season, and returned in 1936 after trying a brief, but barely profitable, spell working on the Tyne. The 46-year-old steamer finally succumbed to the breakers' torches in April 1937, her owners deciding not to go for a third season with their venerable excursion steamer.

The main reason for the defeat of the *Marchioness of Breadalbane* was the arrival of the neat little motor ship *Brit*, completed in time for the 1935 season by Fellows & Company at Great Yarmouth for the local company Longfield Brothers. E. W. & S. H. D. Longfield had previously operated a wooden-hulled launch named *Britannia* out of Yarmouth until she was replaced by the first *Brit* in 1928 (the name *Britannia* having been taken by P. & A. Campbell for its new paddle steamer). The first *Brit* was a steel-hulled motor vessel, some 60 feet long by 16 feet broad. She was displaced by the new *Brit* in 1935, being sold to Mr Albert Butler for use at Bridlington and later Whitby as the *Princess Marina*. In 1952 the *Princess Marina* came south to join Thames Launches' fleet at Twickenham to start a new and extensive career on the Thames under a variety of subsequent owners. The new *Brit*, however, was a more substantial vessel, 88 feet long by 19 feet beam, and was quick to take charge at Great Yarmouth, as Tom Machin describes in his book *MV Coronia Diamond Jubilee*:

> 'The brightly painted *Brit* spent five busy seasons operating from Yarmouth's Town Hall Quay during the heady days of the thirties. Starting daily at 10.30am, she would make two 2-hour trips, leaving the quay and heading down river to the open sea, a turn to the north along the coast past the Marine Parade and on to the Britannia Pier to embark more passengers. After embarkation she would set course for the North Scroby Elbow. Running along the sandbanks her

Above The *Marchioness of Breadalbane* (1890): as the postcard says, 'sailing from South Pier, Lowestoft, daily during summer'.

Below Fellows & Company's first *Brit* (1928) was a pioneer motor excursion ship at Great Yarmouth.

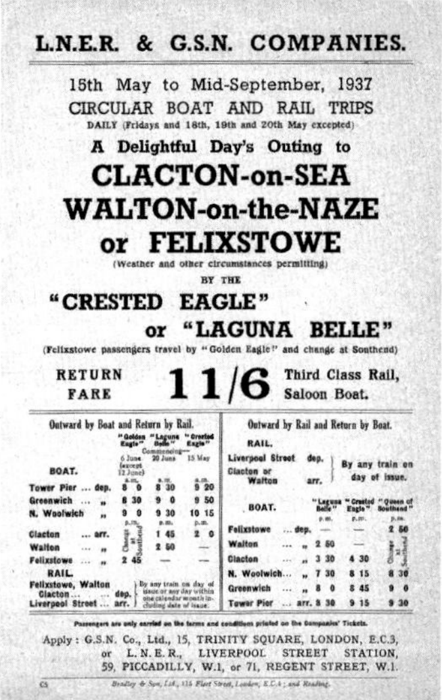

L.N.E.R. & G.S.N. COMPANIES.

15th May to Mid-September, 1937
CIRCULAR BOAT AND RAIL TRIPS
DAILY (Fridays and 18th, 19th and 20th May excepted)

A Delightful Day's Outing to
CLACTON-on-SEA
WALTON-on-the-NAZE
or FELIXSTOWE
(Weather and other circumstances permitting)

BY THE
"CRESTED EAGLE"
or "LAGUNA BELLE"
(Felixstowe passengers travel by "Golden Eagle" and change at Southend)

RETURN FARE **11/6** Third Class Rail, Saloon Boat.

Outward by Boat and Return by Rail.

BOAT.	"Golden Eagle" Commencing— 6 June (except 12 June)	"Laguna Belle" 20 June	"Crested Eagle" 15 May
	a.m.	a.m.	a.m.
Tower Pier ... dep.	8 0	8 30	9 20
Greenwich ... "	8 30	9 0	9 50
N. Woolwich "	9 0	9 30	10 15
	p.m.	p.m.	p.m.
Clacton ... arr.	Change at Southend	1 45	2 0
Walton ... "		2 50	—
Felixstowe ... "	2 45	—	—

RAIL.
Felixstowe, Walton, Clacton ... ... dep. / Liverpool Street ... arr. — By any train on day of issue or any day within one calendar month including date of issue.

Outward by Rail and Return by Boat.

RAIL.
Liverpool Street dep. / Clacton or Walton arr. — By any train on day of issue.

BOAT.	"Laguna Belle"	"Crested Eagle"	"Queen of Southend"
	p.m.	p.m.	p.m.
Felixstowe ... dep.	—	—	2 50
Walton ... "	2 50	—	Change at Southend
Clacton ... "	3 30	4 30	
N. Woolwich... "	7 30	8 15	8 30
Greenwich ... "	8 0	8 45	9 0
Tower Pier ... arr.	8 30	9 15	9 30

Passengers are only carried on the terms and conditions printed on the Companies' Tickets.

Apply: G.S.N. Co., Ltd., 15, TRINITY SQUARE, LONDON, E.C.3, or L.N.E.R., LIVERPOOL STREET STATION, 59, PICCADILLY, W.1, or 71, REGENT STREET, W.1.

CS Bradley & Son, Ltd., 115 Fleet Street, London, E.C.4; and Reading.

passengers could view the basking seals. On returning to the pier, passengers who wished could disembark before she steamed back into the river and up to the Town Hall Quay. Evening trips were usually south to Lowestoft Ness. The fares for all sailings were 2/-.'

Other excursion ships were those of the Yarmouth & Gorlestone Steamboat Company, whose larger vessels were the *Norwich Belle*, *Hotspur* and *Oulton Belle*.

An interesting new adventure for GSN's *Royal Eagle* in 1935 was her attendance at the Royal Naval Review at Spithead. This was repeated at the Naval Review in 1937. She also attended the maiden voyage departure of Cunard Line's *Queen Mary* on 27 May 1936 in the company of the *Queen of the Channel*. The New Medway Steam Packet Company offered a two-day excursion from Southend and Margate leaving on 26 May with an overnight stop at Brighton, where excursionists were put up in a variety of local hotels.

The *Royal Eagle* operated on all three occasions from Southampton. On one occasion it was realised that the Cook had insufficient portions available for the Spithead Review dinner, and a boat had to be dispatched ashore to rendezvous with caterers at Lee-on-Solent. The *Crested Eagle* also steamed round to the Solent for the Coronation Review. Peake reported:

> 'On this occasion the weather was not very kind to us and we smashed some forward saloon windows with heavy seas going round North Foreland and nearly all the stewards were seasick. We managed to get the windows fixed in Southampton and the Review was duly carried out.'

The *Queen of Southend* was taken in hand ready for the 1936 season when the Acorn yard extended her Upper Deck to the stem. However, this made her a little difficult to handle and the proposed conversion of the *Essex Queen* never took place.

Yet another old Scotsman appeared in the south in 1936 when the North Wales steamer *Lady Orme* arrived at Ramsgate to undertake a season of cruises. This was the former David MacBrayne steamer *Fusilier*, which ended her days for that company at Oban looking after the round Mull, Iona and Staffa excursion circuit. When at Ramsgate, the *Lady Orme* was owned by a Blackpool company, which gave her an attractive white hull and red and black MacBrayne-style funnel. The competition made life hard for the veteran and she was returned in 1937 for service in North Wales and given the unlikely name of *Crestawave* before she too became a candidate for recycling.

So pleased was the New Medway Steam Packet Company with its new diesel 'steamer' that a repeat order was placed in time for the 1937 season. Like the *Queen of the Channel*, this ship, which was to be named the *Continental Queen*, was initially to be part-owned by Denny. However, during December 1936 the entire share capital of the New Medway Steam Packet Company was bought out by GSN in a move that took just 24 hours. Plans for the new ship were then radically altered and she was made to be considerably larger than the *Queen of the Channel* with full-length flared-out sponsons, which gave her additional deck space from the Main Deck upward and provided some protection from severe rolling. These alterations increased the price of the vessel

The former David MacBrayne steamer *Fusilier* (1888) served at Ramsgate in 1936 as the *Lady Orme* for one season wearing a MacBrayne-style red and black funnel but with a white hull.

ROYAL SOVEREIGN
LONDON
KEEP OFF
THE LONDON MIDLAND & SCOTTISH RAILWAY
in conjunction with
EAGLE & QUEEN LINE PLEASURE STEAMERS
Continental and Coastal Cruises
(Weather and other circumstances permitting)
By M.V. "Royal Sovereign"
(or other vessel)
SEASON 1937
London (Fenchurch Street, Kentish Town and certain LMS intermediate stations to Barking) (via Tilbury)
TO
MARGATE CALAIS & BOULOGNE
CALAIS
(Via SOUTHEND and MARGATE)
Every SUNDAY and THURSDAY from JUNE 6th to SEPTEMBER 19th inclusive (except THURSDAY, JUNE 10th and SUNDAY, JUNE 20th) Steamer leaving Tilbury on Sundays at 9.0 a.m. and on Thursdays at 8.45 a.m. (For times of train departures from L M S Stations see back of this handbill). Allowing about 3 hours ashore in Calais or about 7 hours in Margate. Leaving Calais on Return Journey at 4.45 p.m. and Margate at 6.45 p.m.
BOULOGNE
(via SOUTHEND and MARGATE)
Every TUESDAY from JUNE 22nd to SEPTEMBER 14th inclusive. Steamer leaving Tilbury at 8.0 a.m. (For times of train departures from L M S stations see back of this handbill) Allowing about 3 hours ashore in Boulogne or about 8 hours in Margate. Leaving Boulogne on Return Journey at 4.30 p.m. and Margate at 7.0 p.m.
Excellent Breakfasts, Luncheons and Teas obtainable on board at reasonable prices
For Fares, Times of Train Connections, and other information see overleaf

Left The *Royal Sovereign* (1937) leaving Tower Pier with her side 'blisters' much in evidence.

Above This company postcard of the *Royal Sovereign* states on the reverse: 'The first sea going passenger vessel to employ side "blisters" to increase the space within the hull and to act as stabilisers to reduce rolling. Built for the Day-cruise cross-channel passenger services of The New Medway Steam Packet Co Ltd from Gravesend, Tilbury, Southend and Margate to Ostend, Calais or Boulogne, during the summer months, with connecting trains from London. The high standard of catering maintained in these cross-channel services is proverbial.'

from the original contract price of £93,400 to £109,573 3s 6d.

Given larger-capacity direct-drive engines than the *Queen of the Channel*, the new ship had a design speed of 21 knots. She was also even more luxuriously fitted out and was reportedly the most comfortable ship operating on the Thames. She was launched on 28 May 1937 with the new name *Royal Sovereign* and was delivered on 9 July. Her passenger certificates permitted 1,333 on cross-Channel work and 1,600 on the Thames estuary above a line between Margate and Clacton. She was perceived to be the ultimate in design and comfort on the Thames.

The success of Captain Shippick's navy, however, had finally come home to roost. GSN had realised that if you cannot beat them then you must buy them out – and GSN's Eagle Steamers and Shippick's Queen Line slowly began to merge their operations. GSN had long been in expansive mood having recently purchased the Liverpool-based Moss Hutchison Line in 1935, so that by 1939 it had a total of 31 subsidiary and associate companies under its control. These ranged from lighter companies to overseas port agents, and freight forwarders to road haulage companies, in a complex web of wholly and partly owned companies (see my *Birds of the Sea*).

A number of changes followed the introduction of the combined Queen Line and Eagle Steamers excursion fleets, although they were still advertised separately. First, the *Royal Daffodil* replaced the old *Isle of Arran* on the docks cruise roster and the latter was withdrawn and scrapped. The *Queen of the Channel*, now displaced by the new *Royal Sovereign*, resumed the East Coast sailings from Yarmouth to Felixstowe and Clacton with a weekly trip to Ostend from Yarmouth. The *Royal Sovereign*'s terminal was moved from Gravesend to Tower Pier. Other changes included upgrading the *Essex Queen* with a full-width fore saloon, and the gradual application of the Eagle Steamers yellow funnel with thin black top to the whole fleet. The new *Royal Sovereign* inaugurated a no-passport Saturday to Monday weekend trip to Ostend, which for 45 shillings included two nights in a local hotel.

The *Crested Eagle* was used as a floating

Table 6: The combined fleets of Eagle Steamers and the Queen Line in 1939

Name	Built	Tons gross	Length (ft)	Speed (knots)	Comments
Thames Queen	1889	522	240	16	Ex-*Yarmouth Belle* 1928, extensively altered 1936, ex-*Queen of Southend* 1938
Laguna Belle	1896	570	249	18	Ex-*Southend Belle*, acquired by GSN 1935 from East Anglian Hotels Ltd
Essex Queen[1]	1897	465	230	16	Ex-*Woolwich Belle* 1922, acquired 1924
City of Rochester	1904	235	160	15	Built for Medway Steam Packet Company
Golden Eagle	1909	793	276	19	
Queen of Kent[1]	1916	798	235	16	Ex-HMS *Atherstone* 1927
Queen of Thanet[1]	1916	792	235	16	Ex-HMS *Melton* 1928
Medway Queen	1924	318	180	15	
Crested Eagle	1925	1,110	300	20	
Royal Eagle	1932	1,538	290	18	Last paddle steamer to be built for GSN
Queen of the Channel	1935	1,030	255	20	First motor ship to be built (for New Medway Steam Packet Company)
Royal Sovereign	1937	1,527	270	21	Ex-*Continental Queen* 1936
Royal Daffodil	1939	2,061	313	21	

[1] Laid up during 1939 season

grandstand during the Coronation of King George VI, while the *Royal Daffodil* was also used as a viewing platform. W. G. Peake takes up the story again:

'In the 1937 season, after the death of King George V came the Coronation of King George VI. As the *Crested Eagle* was originally built to go under London Bridge, it was decided that she should go up river under all the bridges and lay off the Embankment and be used as a grandstand for the Coronation procession. This meant that a huge grandstand was to be built of tubular steel on deck without a fastening to mark her decks. Our naval architect was brought in to work out stability with this huge superstructure and it gave him an anxious time.

As the telescopic funnel had not been dropped for a number of years or the hinged davits worked, work had to be done to prepare these for action. When we eventually steamed up river with the aid of a tug, we never touched a thing, a great credit to everybody, as there was only inches to spare everywhere. The work of the grandstand commenced. I think it seated 800 people and we had rehearsals of heaving alongside at the crucial time. I had to make sure no loose water or oil was in the ship for stability purposes and time my steam raising and fire lighting so there was no possibility of smoke whilst the passengers were in the stand or the procession was passing. The great day came and I am pleased to say everything went splendidly and our passengers had a magnificent view and the rain came down in torrents just after the procession had passed.'

The *Thames Queen* (1896), the final guise of the *Yarmouth Belle*, later *Queen of Southend*.

At the end of the 1937 season the *Royal Daffodil* was withdrawn and sold for demolition. The last season of the two former *Ascot* class minesweepers, the *Queen of Thanet* and *Queen of Kent*, and of the *Essex Queen* (formerly the *Walton Belle*), was in 1938, after which they were laid up pending a decision on their future. The *Queen of Southend* appeared in 1938 with the name *Thames Queen*, more suited to her new role as the PLA docks cruise ship. Also in 1938 the Gravesend call was substituted for Tilbury, with the link from Gravesend by ferry.

The *Royal Eagle* received an all-white hull down to sponson level in the 1939 season, having even been adorned in shades of biscuit during 1935. These colour schemes were attempts to blend the older steamers with the new image of the motor ships. The *Crested Eagle* finally received a solid one-piece funnel. More importantly, 1939 saw the entry into service of the third and largest of the three motor ships, the *Royal Daffodil*, maintaining the famous name of the former Wallasey ferry sold the year before.

The *Royal Daffodil* had been ordered in the name of the New Medway Steam Packet Company, although on delivery she was registered under the ownership of GSN. The contract stipulated that she was to be wider than the *Royal Sovereign* in order to reduce rolling, she was to have a long straight part of the hull amidships to assist mooring at Margate Pier, she should be able to carry 290 tons deadweight with a draft of 8½ feet, and was to be able to attain 20¾ knots.

The new ship had geared diesels that allowed manoeuvring without stopping and restarting the engines. She also had two funnels, which gave her a more businesslike appearance than the *Royal Sovereign*. She had one-class accommodation for 2,396 passengers and could seat 286 diners in two separate dining rooms. The new *Royal Daffodil* was delivered on 23 March 1939 at a total cost of £135,660, just £1,258 3s 0d over budget. The new ship was an instant, if short-lived, success on the continental services and no-passport overnight excursions.

Any idea that the name 'Royal Daffodil' might have logically reverted to Wallasey Ferries, which in 1934 had been obliged to commission its new ferry *Royal Daffodil* with the suffix 'II', had clearly never occurred to GSN. Captain Shippick, who was displaced from his role of Managing Director when GSN took over the New Medway Steam Packet Company in 1936, wrote of this with obvious pride in a letter to *Sea Breezes* in February 1958:

> 'A few years after the [Great] War the *Royal Daffodil* was for sale, and I purchased her for the New Medway Steam Packet Company which I formed, and steamed her from Liverpool to Rochester to run her on the Sheerness-Southend service, on which she ended her days, but her good name was preserved. When my company, of which I was the Managing Director, was taken over by the General Steam Navigation Company they built the now famous twin-screw passenger motor ship *Royal Daffodil* capable of carrying 2,000 passengers daily from Gravesend, Southend and Margate to France and Belgium.'

This final season of peace supported ten excursion ships on the Thames, all operated by GSN under the Eagle Steamers and Queen Line banners, and there were three old steamers at rest in the docks. Throughout the 1930s the Eagle Steamers stalwarts, the *Golden Eagle* and *Crested Eagle*, had continued unassumingly to ply their trade. In addition to the big ships, the New Medway Steam Packet Company owned three little river launches that ran to Upnor and Allington. They were the *HRH Princess May*, *New Medway* and *Rochester City Belle*. At Southend the *New Prince of Wales* and the *Southend Britannia* continued to ply their trade from their respective jetties adjacent to the Kursaal.

Captain Leonard Horsham, the post-Second World War captain of the *Medway Queen*, had been appointed master of the *City of Rochester* in 1937. In his obituary, which was published in August 1969 in *Paddle Wheels*, H. Collard Stone reported:

> 'The last occasion he [Captain Horsham] took the *City of Rochester* down the River Orwell was a historic one. On Sunday 27 August 1939, when the *City of Rochester* left Ipswich on her usual summer service run, she had more passengers than usual. It was obvious that war was imminent, and many came because they feared that it might be the last of such trips that they would enjoy. This was indeed the case, for on the next day the *City of Rochester* was recalled to her base in the Medway, and since then not a single paddler has punched the waters of the River Orwell. At the same time he [Captain Horsham] can claim to have berthed the last pleasure steamer alongside both Felixstowe Town Pier and Walton-on-the-Naze Pier.'

10. AT WAR AGAIN

'The ship was anchored in the deep channel outside Dunkirk harbour, and all the crew not immediately occupied were transfixed, standing on the blacked-out ship in silhouette one moment then reflected in the flashes of bombs and gunfire the next. Everyone seemed awe stricken and no wonder. The scene was one to which we returned six further times, and I shall never ever forget it. The unexpected sight of every British craft imaginable, from single rowing boats to destroyers which rallied to Dunkirk at that time – the fierce opposition by the enemy. Mixed emotions of fear, horror, wonder and pride fought for supremacy inside me as I gazed out, swallowing a huge lump in my throat.'
From an article by Thomas Russell, Chief Cook aboard the minesweeper *Medway Queen* at Dunkirk, *Sea Breezes*, February 1970

Over the three days prior to the declaration of war on 3 September 1939 some 20,000 children were evacuated by sea from the capital to reception areas in Felixstowe, Lowestoft and Great Yarmouth, the threat of German air raids being immediate and real. The children were processed at the three ports and sent on to live their war in rural areas or provincial towns away from the horrors of the air bomb. Many more children, of course, were evacuated by rail. The vessels engaged in this work were the *Royal Eagle*, *Crested Eagle*, *Golden Eagle*, *Laguna Belle*, *Royal Daffodil*, *Royal Sovereign*, *Queen of the Channel* and *Medway Queen*. The bridge fronts of each vessel were hastily lined in wood cladding and each master was issued with a firearm.

Press pictures of children at Greenwich waiting to board the *Royal Eagle* show a happy and smiling crowd, eagerly setting off on their first expedition without their parents. Each was labelled with his or her name and approximate destination. Most were placed with families together with siblings or school friends, but some found themselves in more isolated placements while others ended up in far from welcoming situations.

Southend Pier took on a new role, immediately becoming the operations centre for the Thames approaches and in due course for the East Coast convoys, with a number of the Sun Tugs fleet available as tenders. Stories of horror are numerous – for example, the single-line-ahead convoy coming up to the Southend Anchorage as a German bomber picked each off, missing just one, presumably as the bomb discharge mechanism failed.* There was valour too, of the seaman who shinned up the flag mast on the pier to retrieve the halyard, which had been dropped by the signalman in poor conditions in the middle of an air raid. And there was happiness: the two ratings at the back of the church parade turning left to attend to a quiet game of chess as the rest of the column turned right into the church porch!

It did not take long for the Thames steamers to be requisitioned for duty. The two former minesweepers *Queen of Kent* and *Queen of Thanet* quickly reverted to their former naval roles, initially based at Dover but later transferred to the Forth. The *Essex Queen* was converted for use as an emergency hospital ship under the command of her peacetime master Captain William G. Braithwaite, while the *Laguna Belle* became an ambulance ship, also on the Thames.

* The author's father was the naval signalman aboard the one surviving collier: 'We saw the bombs fall on the column ahead of us and as the ship in front of us was hit we counted, the necessary 10 seconds passed and, as we got to 20, the ship behind us went up.'

The *Royal Daffodil* (1939) was one of the many excursion ships used to evacuate children from the London area in the three days prior to the outbreak of war.

The *Thames Queen* and the *Royal Eagle* were fitted out for anti-aircraft duties and served initially on the Thames, the *Royal Eagle* acting as Thames flagship. Her soda fountain became the stoker petty officers' mess, the tea room the sick bay, and the grill room the seamen's mess deck. During her 2½-year commission as ack-ack ship HMS *Royal Eagle*, a total of 629 days were spent at sea and she engaged 52 enemy aircraft. It was as an ack-ack ship that the *Royal Eagle* discovered that the old GSN boast that she was the fastest paddle steamer in the world was untrue. For some reason, a race developed with fellow ack-ack flotilla member the *Jeanie Deans**, built for the London & North Eastern Railway's Craigendoran-based Clyde fleet of steamers in 1931. The *Royal Eagle* lost.

The effectiveness of the anti-aircraft ships is encapsulated in a small piece of text taken from an article by D. D. Hutchings describing a three-month period during which he served aboard the *Thames Queen* in the winter of 1942. The article first appeared in *Paddle Wheels*, Summer 1972:

> 'I am afraid that if we did shoot it was when anything came near, as we had no means of identifying any aircraft, but we apparently never hit anything. Anchored with any swell, the sponsons were hit from underneath by waves and the whole ship shook. About 100 of us lived aboard, and in 24 hours our fresh water was all used. I can still remember that our captain was Captain Horsham. He knew all the channels between the sandbanks off the East Coast without having to refer to charts. When loaded with water and ammunition the *Thames Queen* waddled out of harbour with a considerable list.'

The *Royal Sovereign* was taken to war by her peacetime master, Captain Tommy Aldis. The ship assumed the name HMS *Royal Scot* on being taken over by the Navy in 1940, to avoid confusion with the battle cruiser HMS *Royal Sovereign*. Tommy Aldis was a modest and quiet man, but he was eventually persuaded to recount a summary of his war aboard the *Royal Sovereign* in *Paddle Wheels*, Winter 1974:

> 'We started by evacuating all the children and expectant mothers from Dagenham and

* The *Jeanie Deans* ended her commercial life on the Thames as the *Queen of the South* for the 1966 and 1967 seasons (see Chapter 12).

The *Royal Eagle* (1932), still with the black spread-eagle emblem on the forward superstructure, despite wartime camouflage. *Imperial War Museum*

Gravesend to Great Yarmouth. From there we were put on the British Expeditionary Force from Southampton and Cherbourg; after that we were taken over by the Fleet Air Arm, doing exercises from positions off the Isle of Wight area, being dive-bombed and torpedoed; then we were sent to Troon in Scotland, doing the same thing, but unfortunately that didn't last, and the Dunkirk job came along, so back we came and did nine trips, bringing from Dunkirk some 16,000 troops to Margate.

After a short spell at Southampton, we then were sent with troops on a new expeditionary force to St Malo. On arriving it was found that the hospital ship had not arrived which was due to take some 1,000 troops who had been injured from an ammo train which the Germans had bombed so we were made into the hospital ship. After arriving and disembarking the troops we were then sent to Cherbourg to take all the troops that were retreating. After this operation we were sent to the Tail of the Bank, Scotland, to be put on a swivel mooring up on the Gareloch.

From there we went south again to be taken over by the Navy and do duties in the Thames estuary. On passage from Scotland to Cardiff we were sunk by an acoustic mine in the Bristol Channel; 32 of us badly injured and one killed, my Chief Officer. That briefly was the *Royal Sovereign*'s war service.'

That the sinking of the *Royal Scot* (*Royal Sovereign*) took place on 9 December 1940 demonstrates how intense the early months of the war had been. This was also the period of the blitz, the lightning war, in which the German air raids were designed to cripple industry, communications, docks and cities. The sailor home from active service on leave turns the corner into his street to find a pile of rubble where once his house and family had been...

The evacuation of Dunkirk, the 'Dunkirk job' that Captain Aldis alluded to, was carried out by ships large and small – even the cockle bawlies from Leigh-on-Sea were requisitioned for use. The Thames steamers involved other than the *Royal*

The *Royal Sovereign* (1937) disembarking troops of the 2nd Royal Inniskilling Fusiliers together with a 40mm Bofors gun at Cherbourg on 16 September 1939. *Imperial War Museum*

Sovereign were the paddle steamers *Royal Eagle*, *Crested Eagle*, *Golden Eagle*, *Queen of Thanet* and *Medway Queen*, the motor ships *Queen of the Channel* and *Royal Daffodil*, and even the little wooden-hulled Southend excursion ships *Southend Britannia* and *New Prince of Wales* (see Chapter 7). The smaller ships were put in the charge of junior naval officers, and this, as it happened, was the undoing of the *New Prince of Wales*. Not realising that her engines were fuelled by paraffin, the officer topped up the fuel tanks with diesel, causing the vessel to stall several times on the outward trip until the engines eventually failed to restart and she drifted inshore towards La Panne to be bombed and sunk.

In my GSN history, *Birds of the Sea*, I wrote:

> 'The pioneer motor ship *Queen of the Channel* and the *Crested Eagle* were both lost at Dunkirk and very nearly also the brand new *Royal Daffodil*. The *Queen of the Channel* was bombed and sunk although all on board were taken off, but the bombing of the *Crested Eagle* set her fuel oil alight and only 150 men were able to get clear of the vessel, many with serious burns. The *Royal Daffodil* survived a bomb alongside her port engine room. Taking on a serious list, she was able to limp home, where temporary repairs were effected, repairs that in the event carried her through the war. She had made seven return trips accounting for 9,000 men. The smaller *Medway Queen* also made seven trips and retrieved just over 3,000 troops, while the *Royal Eagle* was able to make three trips with 1,000 aboard on each return journey.'

The *Medway Queen* was then attached to the Dover Patrol of the 10th Flotilla of Minesweepers, together with the *Queen of Kent*. The Chief Cook aboard the *Medway Queen* was Thomas Russell, and in his previously quoted *Sea Breezes* article he recalled how he had to feed 3,000 men over a three-day period from his small galley and coal-fired range:

Above One of the survivors of Dunkirk – and of two World Wars – was the *Golden Eagle* (1906).

Below The little *New Prince of Wales* (1923), seen in happier days, was a Dunkirk victim – her paraffin engines failed after her tanks had been topped up with diesel.

'I swayed on sore feet, my head ached abominably and my body was racked with fatigue as up until then I had had no sleep for 72 hours. The month of May 1940 was waning and the wartime evacuation of Dunkirk was in full swing. It was 4.00am.

The end of a bandage was dripping in the mess tin which was held out to me, but I was unable to stop my dip-and-pour rhythm in time to avoid emptying a ladle of stew over it. Curiosity made me look up and some drops of perspiration fell from the end of my nose into the stew. The soldier I saw was wounded in the head, his young face pinched and white under the blood-soaked field dressing. Blood and sweat. They were certainly fitting symbols of the harrowing event we were experiencing and the manner of its achievement.

Our eyes met as, reaching out, he removed the bandage then heartily sucked the gravy from the end of it before tucking it back in place. It was a savage gesture and I wondered when he had eaten last. He grinned at me, as if it hurt his lips to stretch them. "Thanks pal, tastes smashing."'

The *Laguna Belle* (1896) seen towards the end of her commercial career under GSN ownership (*above*), and as an anti-aircraft vessel; she was to be deemed not fit for further service after the war.

Amongst all this the *Medway Queen* was able to rescue the crew of P. & A. Campbell's steamer, the *Brighton Belle*, when she was wrecked off Dunkirk on 28 May. After three days' leave for crew and ship, the *Medway Queen* reverted to minesweeping duties. When the paddle minesweepers of the Dover Patrol were replaced in 1942, the *Medway Queen* alone was retained and became a 'sweeper training ship', although she was later transferred to the Tyne, only being released from service in 1947.

Life for the *Royal Daffodil* also calmed down a bit when she was dispatched to the Larne to Stranraer ferry route until 1944, although in late February 1941 she had to put to sea in a heavy gale to rescue the crew of a sinking flying boat. Her running mate from 1943 onwards was the P. & A. Campbell steam turbine excursion ship *Empress Queen*, which had been given an 'Eagle' name, the *Queen Eagle*, while she served in the anti-aircraft flotilla on the Thames together with the *Royal*

Eagle and the *Thames Queen* in the early part of the war.

In 1945 the *Royal Daffodil* came south to help maintain the leave boat service from Dover. She was finally released from this in June 1947, almost two years after the war had ended.

By contrast the *City of Rochester* was never able to contribute to the war effort. Conversion work carried out at the Acorn yard to turn her into a minesweeper was abandoned at a late stage, and instead she was turned into a naval store vessel. On 19 May 1941, the eve of her departure from Rochester, she was so severely damaged by a nearby bomb blast when an enemy parachute mine went off that she was later beached and her metalwork salvaged.

The *Essex Queen*, which had served as an emergency hospital ship, largely on the Thames, was released in December 1945. She was immediately sold to the South Western Steam Navigation Company at Totnes and given the name *Pride of Devon*. However, after the 1949 season she was laid up and later sold for demolition. The *Laguna Belle* was released in 1945 and she too was sent to the breakers in 1946, as was the *Thames Queen* when she was released in 1947, neither being deemed fit for further civilian service. Thus the last of the 'Belle' steamers were taken away, the *Essex Queen* being the former *Walton Belle*, the *Laguna Belle* the former *Southend Belle*, and the *Thames Queen* formerly the *Queen of Southend* and before that the *Yarmouth Belle*.

Gone too were the motor ships *Queen of the Channel* and *Royal Sovereign*, and the paddle steamers *Crested Eagle* and *City of Rochester*. The survivors were the motor ship *Royal Daffodil*, and the five paddle steamers *Golden Eagle*, *Royal Eagle*, *Medway Queen*, *Queen of Thanet* and *Queen of Kent*. All waited patiently to be reconditioned and put back in service. They were in lamentable condition, having barely been serviced during the war years, although the *Golden Eagle* is recorded as one of the largest vessels to have been dealt with at Cosens's ship repair yard at Weymouth during the war.

Although the Southend-based passenger vessel *New Prince of Wales* had been lost at Dunkirk, the other wooden-hulled Southend boat, the *Southend Britannia*, had survived unscathed. She had been used as a naval leave boat and tender, and as she had been little altered for this role she was able to resume services from her Southend jetty in 1946, initially just to Sheerness and back. She was subsequently sold for service on the Colne with the name *Brightlingsea Belle*, and later operated out of Brixham as *Western Lady V*. In 1960 she was bought by Thames Television and moored alongside its studios below Teddington Lock as a hospitality ship and floating restaurant. With her engines removed, she was renamed the *Iris*. Sold for scrap in 1987, her timbers having taken their toll over the 63 years since her construction, the *Iris* was towed away for scrap. Resold again, she re-emerged as the Thames houseboat *Beverley*, a role she maintained for several more years.

The Southend Motor Navigation Company, owner of the *New Prince of Wales*, which had cost £11,000 to build in 1923, was offered just that same amount of compensation after the war in 1946. Thorneycroft at Woolston, which had built the ship, quoted a figure nearer ten times that for a replacement. The owner, which had also lost one of its smaller motor boats at Dunkirk, was left to struggle on, finally closing its books in 1970.

Damage to the Thames piers and the dock system had been extensive. With the terror of the war now over, the grey and austere post-war period was characterised by shortages – of food, of clothing and of materials. Rehabilitation of the Thames steamers and their piers was not an immediate priority.

An article that first appeared in *Paddle Wheels*, Winter 1974, recalling the long service of Captain Tommy Aldis, concludes:

> 'It was on 8 June 1946 that the first two post-war pleasure steamers sailed into Margate, a most fitting occasion as the nation was celebrating Victory in Europe Day. There was one person and ship in particular who should have received a hero's welcome – the *Queen of Thanet*, again with Captain T. J. Aldis DSC at the helm, first to come alongside. Standing there on the navigating bridge, his thoughts must have gone back to the 4,500 souls he landed there during the darkest days of the war; and had it not been for deeds such as these, we trippers might never again have been aboard. Fitting enough, following in our wake, was another Dunkirk veteran, the *Royal Eagle*.'

11. THE END OF EAGLE STEAMERS

Things began to look up considerably after the first post-war summer of 1946, when only the *Queen of Thanet* and *Royal Eagle* were in service. The *Medway Queen* was extensively refurbished and converted back to her peacetime configuration at Northam in Southampton. She was put under the command of Captain Leonard Horsham and was ready to resume the early 1947 summer schedule between Strood Pier and Southend. One by one the surviving ships reappeared, many of them being serviced and refurbished at the Acorn yard at Rochester. The *Queen of Thanet* and *Queen of Kent*, now with only foremasts, took up cruises from Southend, Clacton and Margate. The *Golden Eagle* was placed on the Tower Pier to Southend and Clacton route, although the Wallet Channel had badly silted up during the war and an extra 30 minutes had to be scheduled for the journey to Clacton for most states of the tide. The *Royal Daffodil*, still nursing her damaged portside engine, was on non-landing French coast cruises, which started at Gravesend and called at Southend and Margate.

The so-called 'overland' passage to Margate, close along the Kent coast, remained out of bounds due to the danger of wreckage and uncleared mines. This remained the case until the 1949 season. Sheerness Pier, which had been cut in two as a security measure, was recommissioned in time for the 1948 Medway schedule, when Herne Bay was also reopened to traffic.

It was also in 1946 that the Thames Waterbus service was introduced. This provided a regular service between Putney and Greenwich calling at Cadogan, Lambeth, Charing Cross, Tower,

A survivor of two World Wars, the *Queen of Kent* (1916) once more looks the part in civilian clothes complete with the New Medway Steam Packet white horse emblem on her funnels.

Cherry Garden, Wapping and Limehouse. It was inaugurated using a series of smart diesel vessels such as the *Festival*, some 85 feet in length and carrying up to 250 passengers. R. G. Odell was a major stakeholder in the service. It survived for a number of years but was eventually overtaken by the modern-day tourist boats, bateaux mouches and the fast commuter services; nowadays the latter seem to come, and later fail, on a regular basis.

The 1947 summer was not only exciting because of the resumption of near normal schedules, but also because a competitor dared to rear its head. This was The Three Star Shipping Company, which had purchased the former Admiralty yacht and patrol vessel *Enchantress* and rebuilt her as the luxury day excursion vessel *Lady Enchantress*. Bought for just £22,500, conversion work at Thorneycroft's yard at Woolston came to a staggering £174,000, and that had been reduced from a higher figure after considerable haggling – the owners of the new company were three actors, hence The Three Star Shipping Company. Nonplussed, they put their newly refurbished turbine steamer on a basic Gravesend to Southend and Margate roster, starting on 4 August with cruises towards France or along the Kent coast. The *Lady Enchantress* carried out 33 trips in a six-week season; with a fare of only 7s 6d, undercutting GSN by 5 shillings on the French coast cruise, she was extremely popular.

Having been designed originally as the sloop HMS *Bittern*, the narrow beam of the *Lady Enchantress* gave her an unfortunate tendency to pitch even in the slightest sea. Quite a number of passengers were perturbed by the motion of the ship and would not contemplate a repeat booking, which made her longer-term viability questionable.

Six weeks was not nearly enough to begin to recoup the financial outlay, and the ship was laid up at Gravesend in mid-September with virtually no prospect of a return the next season. Throughout 1948 she lay at Denton below Gravesend, but was eventually refitted at Southampton for excursion duties at Torquay, divided between long day cruises to Guernsey and shorter coastal cruises. She commenced service on 10 August 1950 and ended her career dramatically on 31 August with the radio message:

The *Lady Enchantress* (1934), registered in Ramsgate, is seen while in dry dock at Southampton.

> '*Lady Enchantress* position lat 49° 50' north, long 2° 45' west, forward boiler out of action, brickwork now failed completely. After brickwork now failed, refractory casing white hot, proceeding at about 40 revolutions almost stopped. Request tug to tow into port. Weather good at present, passengers comfortable.'

She arrived back in Torquay the following afternoon behind the Admiralty tug *Turmoil*. Her place at Torquay on the Guernsey and coastal excursions was taken the following year by P. & A. Campbell's *Empress Queen*.

The year 1948 saw the zenith of the post-war services. The highlight was the entry into service of a new *Royal Sovereign*, built by Denny to replace her namesake lost in the war. Her maiden voyage from London to Ramsgate took place on 24 July. Frank Burtt described the new ship as follows:

'...trial speed 20.5 knots, gross tons 1,850, passenger accommodation 1,783. The propelling machinery consists of two sets of 12-cylinder Sulzer engines. The Main Deck has two dining saloons seating 96 and 140 diners respectively. The Promenade Deck has a smoke room, there is also a sun lounge 145 feet by 33 feet and a covered observation lounge 40 feet in length. With the exception of the main engines, everything is electrically operated.'

From the mid-1947 season all the GSN boats started to carry the company house flag on their otherwise plain yellow funnels, while the *Medway Queen*, *Queen of Thanet* and *Queen of Kent* all began to wear the white prancing horse (Invicta of Kent) house flag of the New Medway Steam Packet Company. The new *Royal Sovereign* was adorned with the GSN flag on her funnel from the outset. This addition enhanced the appearance of the *Royal Daffodil*, whose plain pre-war funnels looked comparatively thin and gaunt, but the *Golden Eagle* and *Royal Eagle*, which both retained thin black tops to their funnels, as well as sporting the new emblem, never quite looked right. This new livery followed the trend from the late 1930s when the GSN flag was applied to the black funnels of the company's Mediterranean traders in order to distinguish them from their Moss Hutchison Line counterparts.

The *Royal Eagle* displaying the GSN house flag on her funnel.

Two smaller second-hand vessels also joined the combined fleets, which now traded as Eagle Steamers and the New Medway Steam Packet Company (rather than the Queen Line), even though all were wholly owned by GSN. The two new motor ships were the *Crested Eagle*, which was bought for the docks cruises, and the *Rochester Queen*, which was bought for the Medway ports to Herne Bay route, one each for Eagle Steamers and the New Medway Company. The *Crested Eagle* started on 2 June from Tower Pier, initially carrying schoolchildren to the Royal Victoria dock system with one public cruise on Saturdays only, but increased to three a week by July. The pedigree of the little ship was described in a review article in *Sea Breezes* in August 1948:

'The present *Crested Eagle* is a small motor ship built in 1938 by Messrs John Crown of Sunderland as the Scarborough passenger vessel *New Royal Lady*. She was designed for the Yorkshire coast excursions and was owned by Messrs Thomas Round & Sons. After the war the first word of her name was dropped and, under the ownership of John Hall (Cruises) of Granton, she was used on day trips on the Forth.'

The *Crested Eagle* was powered by twin Crossley diesels, giving her a service speed of 13 knots. In keeping with the 1930s mini-liner fashion, she had been built with two funnels, despite her diminutive size. Although she had managed to

The *Royal Sovereign* (1948) at Southend on 21 August 1962. *Author*

The main Dining Saloon aboard the Royal Sovereign (above), and the Lounge Deck and Cocktail Bar.

The Scarborough excursion ship *New Royal Lady* (1938) replaced the *Royal Lady*. She later had her side alleyways plated in to become the *Crested Eagle*, seen in the second photograph having just left Tower Pier.

keep her forward funnel throughout the war as a patrol boat and while on the Forth (where it was used as the bar store), GSN promptly removed it to increase deck space; consequently her remaining funnel always looked to be too far aft. The licensed passenger capacity of the new *Crested Eagle* was 672 on the Thames.

The *Rochester Queen* was an ex-military vessel, and in her new civilian guise she was licensed to carry 425 passengers. Her pedigree is described in *Ferry Powerful* (see References) as follows:

'A number of interesting small diesel-powered passenger vessels was converted from military use in post-war years. One of these was the New Medway Steam Packet Company's excursion ship *Rochester Queen*, which was built in 1944 as LCG(M) *181*; another was the *Sark Coast* of the Coast Lines' fleet, which was built in 1945 as LCG(M) *196*. Both ships were former "Landing Craft Guns", and were converted by Bolsons of Poole for civilian use in 1948. As these landing craft were originally fitted with fairly large guns, there was a need to ballast them to obtain sufficient stability to cater for the guns' weight, as well as the recoil from a shot fired broadside. For this, the ships had a large floodable double bottom, which also provided them with an additional safety factor in civilian life. Given twin Paxman engines, there was saloon accommodation on the Lower Deck, and a central deckhouse containing a lounge. The original transom stern was rounded off, and the bulwarks had an attractive sheer to them.'

With this new tonnage, and a similar but smaller running mate for the *Royal Sovereign* on order at Denny's yard, it was no surprise that the two elderly former *Ascot* class minesweepers, the *Queen of Thanet* and *Queen of Kent*, were placed on the 'for sale' list at the end of the 1948 season. Both were quickly bought by the Southampton, Isle of Wight & South of England Royal Mail Steam Packet Company and respectively renamed the *Solent Queen* and *Lorna Doone*. They provided useful stop-gap tonnage on the South Coast even though they were soon displaced and scrapped due to deteriorating hull plates and associated costs of repair, the *Solent Queen* in 1951, following a fire, and her sister the following year.

The last of the purpose-built motor ships from Denny's yard at Dumbarton was a new *Queen of the Channel*. Replacing her namesake lost at Dunkirk, she was registered under the ownership of GSN, but initially wore the colours of the New Medway Steam Packet Company, with the white horse on her funnel. The new ship had a certificate for 1,350 passengers and provided all the facilities that her slightly larger sister the *Royal Sovereign* could boast save for the Upper Deck lounge, but with 1 foot less draft and a slightly lower speed of 19 knots. She was delivered on 25 May in time for the 1949 summer season. Fleet deployment in 1949 was as follows:

Royal Daffodil: Gravesend to Southend and Margate and cruise to off Cap Gris Nez
Queen of the Channel: Ramsgate-based cruises
Royal Sovereign: Tower Pier to Margate direct and sea cruise
Royal Eagle: Tower Pier to Southend, Margate and Ramsgate
Golden Eagle: Tower Pier to Southend and Clacton
Crested Eagle: Tower Pier to London Docks, or Gravesend and Southend with short sea cruise
Medway Queen: Rochester and Chatham to Southend
Rochester Queen: Strood to Southend and Herne Bay

This, however, was not to last, as E. C. B. Thornton recounts in his book *Thames Coast Pleasure Steamers*:

'One gets the distinct impression that the GSN was embarrassed by excess tonnage and took steps to rectify this. The *Golden Eagle* was not commissioned in 1950 and the company found that the running of two vessels from Tower Pier to Margate was not justified. The season was opened with the *Royal Daffodil* running from Tower Pier to Margate via Southend, to be relieved in mid-June by *Royal Sovereign*. The *Queen of the Channel* performed the Tower Pier to Southend and Clacton service vice *Golden Eagle*. The *Royal Eagle* came into service at the end of June and for the first time in her life did not go on the Tower Pier to Ramsgate run, but instead she took over the Tower Pier to Southend and Clacton service from the *Queen of the Channel*. The latter returned to Ramsgate for the [non-landing] cross-Channel and coastal cruises. However, this did not last for the season for, after 10 August 1950, the *Queen of the Channel* again took over the Tower Pier to Southend and Clacton service from the *Royal Eagle*, which was forthwith laid up.'

Both the *Golden Eagle* and the *Royal Eagle* were dispatched to isolation in Whitewall Creek adjacent to Upnor Woods on the Medway. The isolation of the two silent ships was watched by passengers aboard the *Medway Queen* and the *Rochester Queen* as they passed by. While the elderly *Golden Eagle* went to Grays to be scrapped in mid-1951, GSN kept the *Royal Eagle* on the sale list in the hope that someone could find further work for her. This was not to be, and eventually in November 1953 she too was towed across to Ward's scrapyard at Grays.

Chris Robins remembers the *Medway Queen*

It was the early 1950s, I was 7 or 8, when the family took the train down the pier to board the *Medway Queen* for the trip across the estuary to Herne Bay. Although my favourites were the three big white ships of the GSN fleet, the *Medway Queen* was special too, even though she was so small. As we looked down on the paddle steamer coming alongside the pier head, I was aware of a small, squat, dark grey naval vessel anchored downstream of the pier. My father told me this was a Royal Navy corvette acting as Guardship to four American battle cruisers which were on a courtesy visit to the Thames and lying two-by-two downstream in the Southend Anchorage. These were huge ships – sleek, bristling with armament and painted in a lighter shade of grey than the corvette.

We boarded the *Medway Queen*. There was so much going on and, as always, I was intrigued by the white horse on her tall funnel. The ship was quite crowded when the ropes were cast off and we set sail, not out to sea towards the Kent coast but towards the American visitors. As we approached them most of our passengers surged to the port rail. By the time we came up to the first pair of American battle cruisers, now towering above us, the little *Medway Queen* had taken on an alarming list to port, so much so that the sponsons were dipping into the sea. My father had already taken us to the starboard rail to look over the heads of all the passengers on the port side, from where we got the best view of the visiting ships. The four battle cruisers were impressive, and I remember being particularly struck by the white uniform of their crew.

As we came abreast the first pair of Americans, a sailor lowered our Blue Ensign at the stern. An American seaman on the nearest ship could be seen walking quickly aft in his

Left The **Medway Queen** leaving Southend on 21 August 1962. *Author*

Right Aboard the **Medway Queen**, 25 August 1962. *Author*

posh white uniform, but the deck of the battle cruiser was so long that by the time he got to the American Ensign to lower it in response we were well past the two ships.

Our Captain, I remember, strode across his bridge to look at the submerged paddle, then up hill to starboard to look at the other one now up in the air. 'Would passengers please clear the port rail and move to starboard' was his announcement, and the response soon had the vessel on a more even keel. Of course, that would have been Captain Leonard Horsham himself. It was then that I realised why the Captain had to balance our ship; it was now heeling to port as we turned sharply to starboard on a course that would take us to Herne Bay rather than straight out towards Denmark! The *Medway Queen* would have been unable to turn with all the passengers standing at the port rail, mouths agape at the visitors.

It was then that a deckhand approached my father to confirm that it was he, Mr George Robins, formerly Lieutenant Robins RNVR. 'Sir, the Mate asks that you join him on the Bridge.' The two men quickly disappeared from sight, and at least one whisky later my father emerged to tell mother that 'that was so-and-so, you know, I served with him on the North Sea Convoys'. It was a small world and a world that still lived very much in the shadow of the recent war.

The engine room of the *Medway Queen* was paradise for a small boy, peering over the brass rail into the hot abyss of cranks and eccentrics where the crew no longer looked neat and tidy but appeared hot and sweaty as they tended their machinery with grease gun in one hand and oily rag in the other. The *Medway Queen* rarely rolled in the estuary, but when she had got speed up she would always pitch about the axis of her paddles as the energy from them drove her bows into the water while the buoyancy then pushed the bows up again. This was normal for the paddle steamers, my father told me on his return from the Bridge.

Of course, my little brother Nick was only 2 or 3 years old at the time and will not remember any of this!

The year 1949 was the last that the little *Brit* was to enjoy at Great Yarmouth (see Chapter 9). She was bought in the winter by Thames Launches of Twickenham to operate from the Festival of Britain site adjoining County Hall throughout 1950. She was not entirely suited to the trade on the river and was sold again after the 1950 season to become the *Yorkshire Lady* at Scarborough. She is still working at Scarborough, now with the name *Coronia*.

The 1951 pattern on the Thames was continued for some years: the *Royal Sovereign* on the Tower Pier to Southend and Margate service, the *Queen of the Channel* on the Tower Pier to Southend and Clacton route, and the *Royal Daffodil* on the Gravesend to Southend and Margate run and cruise to off the French coast. In 1952 calls were initiated at North Woolwich by the *Royal Sovereign* and the *Queen of the Channel*, and the *Crested Eagle* was relieved from the PLA Docks cruise roster initially by one of Odell's motor launches and in later years by the PLA tender *St Katharine*. The *Crested Eagle* was placed at Ramsgate for local cruises. In 1953 the *Medway Queen* amalgamated the duties of the *Rochester Queen* with her own, allowing the *Rochester Queen* to go to Clacton to operate her own coastal cruise programme.

The year 1954 saw the reintroduction of cruises to Boulogne for passport holders using the *Royal Daffodil*. The need for passports was relaxed in 1955 when only identity cards were required. The number of no-passport cruises was increased to reflect demand, with the *Queen of the Channel* offering daily Boulogne and Calais trips from either Clacton or Ramsgate in addition to the landing and non-landing cruises operated by the *Royal Daffodil* from Gravesend. The non-landing cruise from Margate was occasionally used to deliver mail and stores to the crew of the Tongue Light Vessel. This required a slow pass down the length of the anchored ship so that packages could be transferred from the Lower Deck passenger door, all to the delight of the excursionists.

The *Royal Sovereign* stuck to her normal Margate roster in 1956. The *Rochester Queen* was scheduled to support the main-line French trips with feeder services from the Medway ports to Southend and Margate, and the *Crested Eagle* ran from Gravesend to Southend and on to Clacton via Swin Spitway. However, at the end of the season the *Rochester Queen* was sold to German owners, although she later came back to the British registry as the *Commodore Queen* in 1961, and later the *Jersey Queen*, before being sold for use as a survey ship off West Africa.

The *Crested Eagle* was chartered to P. & A. Campbell in 1957 and, following a disastrous season on the South Coast, was sold to Magro & Zammit of Malta to become the new Gozo mail and passenger ferry. After lying idle in the St Katharine's Dock for a while, she was delivered to Malta in tow of the Hull tug *Masterman*. Apart from the absence of the two little ships, the basic 1954 service continued through to 1963, with the addition of calls at the newly opened concrete pier at Deal.

Smeaton & Morris, in an unpublished text lodged with DP World in London, report:

The Port of London Authority's steam passenger tender *St Katharine* (1927) undertook the public London Docks cruises in the mid-1950s.

The *Rochester Queen* (1944) seen in a later guise as the *Jersey Queen* at Poole Quay in June 1974. *Author*

'...quite a number of holidaymakers from London ... travelled on a period return ticket and were able to park their baggage in a recognised baggage or left luggage room and thus enjoy the journey to and from their holiday without having to keep guard over suitcases.

The sailings [from Tower Pier] were the bane of road-travelling commuters from the south of London as they led to Tower Bridge being opened one or more times during the height of the morning rush hour; the wise and regular motorist was fully conversant with the sailing programme to beat the bascules!

All vessels had excellent catering facilities with service throughout the day from breakfast through to lunch, high tea and dinner. As many travellers preferred less pretentious surroundings from the very tastefully set-out dining saloons, a cafeteria was also available where the favourite dish was fish and chips. Bars seem to be of paramount importance on all trips, and the licensing laws allowed them to be open all the time the ship was operating, provided she was not alongside the piers for passenger movement.'

In 1963 the veteran paddle steamer *Medway Queen* was still under the command of Captain Horsham, and his Chief Engineer was W. G. E. Ruthven. The vessel operated from Strood Pier to Southend and Herne Bay on Tuesdays, Thursdays and Sundays, to Clacton on Mondays and Wednesdays, and made a double run to Southend

The MacBrayne ferry *Lochinvar* (1908) was little changed but for a yellow funnel when she became the Southend to Sheerness excursion ferry *Anzio I* in 1963.

on Saturdays. However, she was finally withdrawn at the end of the season, after which the New Medway Steam Packet Company ceased to operate passenger ships. The *Queen of the Channel* had forsaken the white horse emblem on her funnel and adopted the GSN house flag several years previously.

A combination of increased costs and the arrival of a competitor hastened the demise of the *Medway Queen* from 1960 onwards. The competitor was the former Fairmile motor launch the *Anzio* (sister of the *Dunkirk* and *Matapan*, both of which remained on service on the South Coast), which came to open a new Southend to Sheerness service in 1960 for Messrs Harvey & Foreman (founded by Mr C. Harvey and Lieutenant Commander W. Foreman). Originally starting in August 1959, the new service was quickly withdrawn due to a demand that the *Anzio* should carry a qualified Thames pilot. She restarted the ferry service on 14 May 1960 and was a huge success. Her four round trips per day often carried near capacity loadings of 198 passengers.

In 1961 she was succeeded by the pioneer passenger motor ship *Lochinvar*, a long-standing member of David MacBrayne's West Highland fleet. Renamed the *Anzio I*, she took up the Sheerness ferry with capacity for 351 passengers. With every passing day she took upwards of 1,000 potential passengers away from the *Medway Queen*, and with every passing day the viability of the paddler became less.

Colin Fleetney described the final arrival of the *Medway Queen* at Strood on her last day of service on 18 September 1963, in an article that first appeared in *Paddle Wheels* in August 1971:

> 'We stayed on deck for another fifteen minutes or so, until we were abeam of the Old Gun Wharf above Chatham Dockyard. Then, descending the forward main companionway, we took up position at the engine room rail, by the fan engine. Here was light, heat and activity. The fan engine, almost at my elbow, throbbed, the oil in its crank case sight glass bobbing gently. The great fan in the main uptake sang, and its steel mesh cage trembled. The main engine, at full power, ran on, cranks whirled, eccentrics tumbled and reversing links nodded. The three engineer officers stood at the controls on the manoeuvring platform, while the rails were crowded with passengers. The steering gear clattered spasmodically and the black greasy links of the steering chains were hauled over the main sprocket wheel, first to port then to starboard.
>
> With a succession of beats which sent the needle oscillating on the dial, the telegraph ordered "Full astern". Soon the hull was pulsating under the power of the plunging rods and gauging cylinders. The orders came down from the bridge fast now, and soon, in between the engine movements we could hear the creak of mooring ropes, and the clatter of bulwarks being thrown open.
>
> The vessel rose and fell, tilted slightly to starboard, righted herself, and was still.

"Stop" rang out, and the engines came to rest, the cranks rocking, the crossheads moving almost imperceptibly on the oily guides. Again and again the telegraph rang, the needle speeding from "Full ahead" to "Full astern". The brazen notes clashed with, and for a time drowned, all other sounds. It came to rest finally, as we all knew it would, at "Finished with engines". The *Medway Queen* had arrived home for the last time.'

The Eagle Steamers trio carried on unabated for another three seasons. Changes occurred in 1966 when, for the first time, the *Royal Sovereign* travelled abroad, midweek from both Great Yarmouth and Clacton to Calais. Her traditional Tower Pier to Margate service was retained only on Saturday and Sunday and was operated for her by the *Queen of the Channel*. That ship and the *Royal Daffodil* maintained the Gravesend to Southend, Margate, Deal to Calais or Boulogne trips so that now Eagle Steamers only had a departure from Tower Pier at weekends. The *Royal Daffodil* picked up some early-season work bringing French schoolchildren to London on day trips.

Smeaton & Morris again:

'As the appeal of this type of outing to the travelling public faded, it was the service on the Thames from Tower Pier to Southend, Margate or Clacton that suffered dwindling numbers without the fare structure being able to make operation of the *Royal Sovereign* economic. She was in fact kept in service for some of the concluding seasons with very little hope of profit. On the other hand the type of passenger from Gravesend, Tilbury and Southend on the trips to the continent

From 1st JUNE until 15th SEPT. 1963
DAILY (except Fridays)
No Sailings on Sunday, 16th June & Sunday, 18th August

THE TWIN-SCREW M.V.
"ROYAL SOVEREIGN"
will sail from SOUTHEND PIER
at 12.0 noon
allowing up to TWO HOURS ashore at
MARGATE
The popular Holiday Resort on the Kent coast
SINGLE 12/- Day 15/- Return PERIOD RETURN 20/-
Children under 14 years Half fare; under 3 years, Free
TIMES
Due Margate at 2.0 p.m. Depart Margate at 4.0 p.m.
Back at Southend 6.0 p.m. approx.

Fully Licensed : Restaurant Service : Light Refreshments
SPECIAL RATES FOR PARTIES BOOKED IN ADVANCE

Sailings are subject to weather and other circumstances permitting
FOR CONDITIONS OF CARRIAGE SEE OVERLEAF
EAGLE STEAMERS
PIER HILL, SOUTHEND-ON-SEA Telephone 66597 (May/Sept.)
(P.T.O

The *Royal Daffodil* (1939) leaving Deal on 12 August 1965. *Author*

The *Queen of the Channel* (1949) leaving Deal on 28 August 1966. *Author*

changed quite considerably. At weekends it became the fashion for works parties to make bookings for their annual outings, no doubt stimulated by the favourable bar arrangements coupled with three or four hours ashore in France where traditionally hard liquor could be consumed. This ultimately led to quite a few troublesome incidents on the *Royal Daffodil* and from time to time she received adverse press comment and publicity on this aspect. On the other hand the *Queen of the Channel* was covering similar voyages from Clacton and Thanet where primarily the excursionists were family holiday parties…'

In mid-winter, five days before Christmas Day 1966, came the announcement that Eagle Steamers would cease trading and that the three stalwarts would be put up for sale. A number of compelling reasons why this should be so were stacked up against continuation of the 'butterfly boats'. Not least was the fact that Stena Line of Sweden had introduced its brand-new passenger and car ferry *Stena Naudica*, marketed as 'The Londoner', on a day trip service from Tilbury to Calais (see Chapter 12). 'The Londoner', both in comfort and catering, was far superior to the GSN ships, which were now dogged by numerous stories of drunken and loutish passengers. With an element of spin, the *Sea Breezes* Commentary by Craig J. M. Carter reported in February 1967:

'Commenting on the 1966 season, a company spokesman said it had been "grim". The seamen's strike had affected party bookings and the weather was bad before the season closed in mid-September. In addition, due to the growth of car and coach traffic to the continent by other routes, the popularity of the day cross-Channel trips to Boulogne and Calais had waned in recent years.

The GSN passenger interests will now be concentrated in Normandy Ferries, to be inaugurated by the new vessel *Dragon* between Southampton and Le Havre on 7 July. GSN also holds a major interest in North Sea Ferries, running a nightly service between Hull and Rotterdam.'

The closure of Eagle Steamers' Thames and continental services in favour of a new roll-on, roll-off vehicle ferry service to France reflected a sea change that was taking place in Britain in the

The freighter *Autocarrier* (1948), seen at Dover in July 1968, was a far cry from the excursion ship *Royal Sovereign*, although she retained a passenger certificate that would have allowed excursion work from Dover had the opportunity arisen. *Author*

mid-1960s. The Beatles were in their Cavern, and the new generation was throwing away the old virtues, including the bowler hat and airs of prudishness. The austere years of post-war Britain were over, young people had money to spend and cars to drive, and the pleasure steamer did not fit comfortably into this new world.

So that was that. The *Royal Daffodil* was laid up for a short while in the South West India Dock before she was sent to Bruges for demolition. On Merseyside, Wallasey Ferries celebrated her demise by removing the numerical suffix from their ferry *Royal Daffodil II*. Meanwhile, the *Royal Sovereign* sat at Deptford, while the *Queen of the Channel* took up residence at Rochester. By April 1967 the *Royal Sovereign* was being demolished to Main Deck level and reassembled as a roll-on, roll-off freight ferry for Townsend Ferries at Dover under the ownership of the Stanhope Shipping Company. She emerged as the ugly duckling *Autocarrier*, her owners graciously retaining a passenger certificate for coastal cruising, a certificate that was founded on removable seating saved from her excursion days that could readily be secured to the covered part of the freight vehicle deck. Alas, the cross-Channel freight business was so buoyant that no day cruises were ever carried out. In 1973 she was sold for further service in the Mediterranean to run the Ischia to Naples ferry under the name *Ischia*. The *Queen of the Channel* remained in solitary confinement on the Medway until, in February 1968, she was picked up by the Greeks to become the *Oia* and later the *Leto*, successfully sailing between Piraeus and Mykonos in almost her original form.

The *Queen of the Channel* was scrapped in 1984 and the *Royal Sovereign* in 2007. And so ends the story. But not quite, for a number of the London staff were transferred to Southampton, there to supervise the development of the new Normandy Ferries cross-Channel car and vehicle ferry service with its irritating advertising champion Norman D. Seagull. The experience of the former London-based staff, with sea and land packages developed with the *Royal Daffodil* to places as far afield as Lisbon, was invaluable to the new enterprise. The *Dragon*, registered at Southampton, started service on 29 June 1967, and the *Leopard*, registered at Le Havre, commenced the following year on 19 May. The thrice-weekly unit load service previously

Above Normandy Ferries' brand-new car ferry *Dragon* (1967) commenced service between Southampton and Le Havre on 29 June 1967. *Author*

Below The small cargo vessel *Petrel* (1965) was the last ship ever to fly the GSN house flag when she was sold in 1978.

offered by the *Oriole* was discontinued, while she and her near sister the *Petrel* were later to become the very last of the company's cargo vessels to fly the GSN flag.

For some reason Eagle Steamers had always been popular as a summer occupation for a number of otherwise deep-sea Hebridean seamen. It was not uncommon to hear the quiet clipped speech, typical of the back-ways of Stornoway, coming from the forecastle, only to be drowned under the brash cockney vowels of the passengers and other crew members. The Hebrideans stood little chance of being heard, as John Young's account in *Sea Breezes* of September 1978 surely verifies:

> 'Went on the *Golden Eagle* for a couple of trips, but I couldn't stand the perishing crowds. One night coming 'ome, I was 'elping get the lines ready up for'ad an' I got a poor bleeder wiv an accordion wrapped round the capstan. Didn't 'arf give me a turn, I can tell yer, an' I went back on the tugs after that.'

12. SOME VALIANT ATTEMPTS

The success of the veteran motor ship *Anzio I* on the Southend to Sheerness service came to an abrupt end when the Sheerness port authority withdrew her berth at the end of the 1963 season when a major reconstruction programme was started. The old ship languished at Tilbury Docks for two years until she caught the attention of a new partnership formed between Mr R. J. Jones of Southend and Captain Adam Fotheringham, who, together with others, formed Cromarty Cruises. The intention was to operate the *Anzio I* on excursions between Inverness and Invergordon. Alas, on her delivery voyage, with Captain Fotheringham in charge, she foundered in foul weather off Donna Nook, near the mouth of the Humber, with the loss of her entire crew of 13. The loss of the ship may have been the result of steering failure, as reported in *Sea Breezes* Commentary for June 1966:

> 'The *Anzio I* was first seen by Coastguards at about midnight on 2 April [1966], when the sea was very rough and the strong gale was pushing the ship towards the shore. The Coastguards flashed the international danger signal on a searchlight to the ship; this was answered and for a short time they thought that the master had altered course. Then the ship appeared to turn a complete circle and seconds later had struck the rock-hard sand, turned broadside on to the sea and rolled over.'

In 1965 Stena Line of Gothenburg placed its small passenger and car ferry *Stena Nordica* on a new service between Tilbury and Calais. Marketed as 'The Londoner', she attracted considerable business, so driving another nail into the coffin of Eagle Steamers. The Stena Line history (see References) reports:

> 'The *Stena Nordica* was ... delivered on 30 June 1965. The Frederikshaven traffic [for which she was built] was considered insufficiently large and the *Stena Nordica* was thus moved over to the English Channel, even if she was, for a while, intended for the Nakskov-Kiel route. Stena Line wound up its interests there, however. After a huge welcome party in London, under Tower Bridge [sic], she was put into traffic between Tilbury and Calais under Stena Line's own management, and with the marketing programme name of "The Londoner", which was painted on the ship's sides.'

The non-landing, day return fare was only £2 10s 0d, and passengers were invited to enjoy a modestly priced full Scandinavian smorgasbord. However, in 1966 the *Stena Nordica* was chartered for use on British Rail's Sealink service between Stranraer and Larne. The larger *Prinsessan Christina* of the associate Sessan Line, on charter from Rederi A/B Göteburg-Frederikshaven Linjen, was substituted, recommencing the seasonal service on 1 April 1966. Still under 'The Londoner' banner, the brand-new but smaller *Stena Baltica* took the service in 1967. It was not resumed thereafter, and the *Stena Baltica* was later sold to the Caledonian Steam Packet Company in 1970 for service between Ardrossan and Brodick as the *Caledonia*.

At the end of the 1963 season Mr Don Rose tested the water by chartering the paddle steamer *Consul* from South Coast & Continental Steamers of Weymouth. The *Consul* was operated on the Thames under the banner of New Belle Steamers. She had been built in 1897 for the Devon Steamship Company as the *Duke of Devonshire* and had served a variety of owners before her best-remembered role under Cosens's colours at Bournemouth as the *Consul*. She was given a green

The *Stena Nordica* (1965) alias 'The Londoner'. The rear of this postcard states: 'Sailing every day from Tilbury to Calais, carrying 126 cars and 1,000 passengers at a speed of 17½ knots.'

hull and an all-yellow funnel for the charter on the Thames. She did some trips from Gravesend, some from London, and ran to Southend and Herne Bay and to the Medway – and all that in the one week beginning 15 September. Mr Rose must have judged the venture unsound as New Belle Steamers was not in business the following year, during which the *Consul* spent her final season in service working short cruises out of Weymouth.

The veteran paddle steamer *Consul* (1897) is seen at Weymouth in her final year of service. *Author*

When she was broken up in 1968 she was an incredible 72 years old.

Unsound the venture with the *Consul* may have been, but the experience gained led to an even more ambitious plan in 1965. This was the most valiant attempt of all at reviving steamer services on the Thames, and was again led by Don Rose, this time with a group within the Paddle Steamer Preservation Society, which successfully tendered to purchase the veteran Clyde paddle steamer *Jeanie Deans*. Placed under the ownership of the Coastal Steam Packet Company and given the traditional name *Queen of the South*, it was intended that the ship ply the Thames between Tower Pier, Greenwich and Southend, with extended cruises to Clacton and other piers on selected days. GSN's *Royal Sovereign* had already

The *Queen of the South* (1931), formerly the Clyde steamer *Jeanie Deans*, leaving Southend on 25 June 1967. *Author*

moved to Great Yarmouth, in this its final season, and the *Queen of the South* was intended to fill the gap thus created. And this she did, just. Entering service on Whit Saturday, 28 May 1966, she managed only a few sailings that summer and early the following season.

Although the *Queen of the South* looked magnificent on the Thames, she was suffering boiler problems and was plagued with mechanical failure. Her erratic timetable did little to attract patronage and it was obvious that she was losing considerable sums of her sponsor's money. Debris in the river played havoc with her sophisticated paddle float system and a great deal of money and effort was spent in maintaining the floats.

In August 1967 a writ was nailed to the mast of the *Queen of the South* for non-payment of various bills and dues, and the Admiralty Marshal ordered her sale; she was towed away to an Antwerp scrapyard on 29 December that same year. It was a sad end to a magnificent ship. Built in 1931 for the shallow approaches to Craigendoran Pier, the gateway for the London & North Eastern Railway to the Clyde, the *Jeanie Deans* was a large ship of 839 tons gross. In her youth her three-crank diagonal engines drove her at 18 knots, which enabled her to become the queen of the long-distance cruises round Arran, to Ayr, Girvan and even Ailsa Craig. In the Second World War she acted as a minesweeper and was nearly lost to a mine while serving as an anti-aircraft vessel on the Thames during the blitz. It was then that the *Jeanie Deans* was able to show the *Royal Eagle* which ship was the faster. Post-war she had returned to summer service from Craigendoran, mainly to Bute and on upper Firth cruises.

Laid up in 1964, the *Jeanie Deans* arrived in the Thames in time for the 1966 season. There she was repainted once again in the red, white and black funnel colours of the North British Railway (and in later years the London & North Eastern Railway Clyde steamers), forsaking the colours of the Caledonian Steam Packet Company. Everyone wished the old steamer success, but luck was against the enterprise from the outset. The only consolation was that the failure of the *Queen of the South* opened the way, in later years, for her slightly younger consort, the *Waverley*, to take up the red, white and black funnel colours of her youth again, and so champion the sea-going paddle steamer on the Thames and elsewhere.

The paddle steamer *Waverley* and her smaller consort, the diesel screw-driven former Isle of

Above **The *Waverley* (1946) passing through Tower Bridge on 27 September 2006 en route for Southend and the Medway.** *Author*

Below **The *Balmoral* (1949) is a regular visitor to the Thames during the early months of each summer.** *Author*

Wight ferry *Balmoral*, now maintain a regular schedule of cruises on the Thames during their summer seasons of diverse services from ports around the British coast. Usually the *Balmoral* is present on the Thames in the early summer and the *Waverley* during late summer. Between them they provide the opportunity to relive some of the classic excursions of old with departures from Tower Pier to and from the many estuarine piers where steamers once queued in turn to berth and discharge their eager passengers.

One of the smaller vessels to ply her trade from Tower Pier was the Falmouth passenger vessel *St Gerrans*. She had been commissioned for the St Mawes to Falmouth ferry service in 1927, a service she faithfully maintained until 1968, when she worked two seasons at Eastbourne before coming to the Thames in 1970. Although successful on the Thames, the *St Gerrans* was really too small and slow for the longer-distance cruises, and was returned to excursion duties on the Fal in 1974. Another West Country visitor was the *Torbay Prince*, which ran cruises from Harwich to Ipswich and other destinations in the late 1960s and early 1970s for the Orwell & Harwich Navigation Company.

Other visitors included the Portsmouth and Isle of Wight paddle ferry *Ryde*, which in her pre-retirement phase was chartered to Gilbey's Gin for a week on the Thames in September 1968. The 'Floating Gin Palace' offered a number of cruises promoting her charterer's distinctive beverage to both invited and paying cruise passengers; for the duration her funnel was disfigured with a large Gilbey company red emblem on a white ground. The centrepiece cruise featured a reunion of some of the men that served aboard the *Ryde* during the Second World War, accompanied by the first 500 people who submitted nominations to the *Evening Standard* for their 'Pub of the Year' competition!

Then, in 1969, something quite unique happened in the history of both the Thames and that long-standing and famous excursion steamer operator, P. & A. Campbell Limited – Campbell moved on to the Thames. Using the chartered Scilly Isles ferry *Queen of the Isles*, a few days' trials were spent in September 1968, followed by a full programme of services for the 1969 season. E. C. B. Thornton reported the season as follows:

> 'In 1969 she [the *Queen of the Isles*] sailed from Cardiff via Weston, Ilfracombe, Penzance and Bournemouth to Hastings on 19 and 20 May. She was mostly based on Eastbourne and Hastings, but once a fortnight she came to the Thames empty, on weekends when tides were favourable, as there was a gap of three weeks in July. On these Saturdays she sailed from Tower Pier at 9.00am and, calling at Southend, arrived at Margate at 2.35pm, did a short sea cruise and

The *Ryde* (1937) in her heyday on Portsmouth-Ryde ferry duties in June 1969. *Author*

returned from Margate at 3.50pm to Southend and Tower Pier, due at 9.45pm. She then returned to Southend during the night and sailed from there on Sunday at 9.00am for Calais, arriving there between 1.45 and 2.15pm, returning at 5.00pm, and due back at Southend between 10 and 10.15pm. Then she returned to Hastings. This involved a lot of light sailings virtually from Hastings to Tower Pier and back. She also did some sailings based on Ramsgate and Margate to Ostend. At the end of the season, P. & A. Campbell stated that the South Coast and Thames services would not be repeated in 1970.'

Although the season was successful, it was not particularly lucrative. This may well have been due to the combination of light sailings and the questionable suitability of a vessel with a large cargo capacity used exclusively on day passenger excursion sailings. The *Queen of the Isles* was returned to her owners at the end of the 1969 season, after which she was sold for service in the Pacific.

Campbell had another go a few years later in 1977, using the newly acquired *Devonia*, formerly the *Scillonian* dating from 1956, and former running mate of the *Queen of the Isles* on the Penzance to Scilly Isles ferry. The *Devonia* commenced on 14 July with a 10.00am departure from Tower Pier via Greenwich to Southend. The

Left **The Scilly Isles ferry *Queen of the Isles* (1965) saw brief service on the Thames.** *Author*

Below **The *Scillonian* (1956) ran on the Thames as P. & A. Campbell's *Devonia* for the 1977 season only.** *Author*

season was reported in *Paddle Wheels*, Autumn 1977, as follows:

> 'The Tower Pier to Southend service started with virtually no advance publicity, but loadings picked up encouragingly and the season was extended to 25 September mainly due to party bookings. The *Devonia* operated daily except Mondays, and on four afternoons there was also an estuary cruise out of Southend, which proved extremely popular. Although there was a couple of minor mishaps including a mid-August failure in one engine, and later a collision with a dumb barge, the *Devonia* completed the season without problems, having no difficulty in maintaining the 3 hours and 40 minutes schedule to Southend.'

P. & A. Campbell's Thames services were not resumed thereafter. The *Devonia* was used on the Bristol Channel in 1978, then sold for use at Torquay as the *Devoniun* and resold for service as a ferry between Invergordon and the Orkneys under the name *Syllingar*, Norse for 'Scilly Isles', ceasing in 1985.

While all these short-lived forays on to the Thames had been proceeding, a more substantial development was taking place on the Medway. The preservation of the former river excursion steamer *Kingswear Castle* was gathering pace, with talk of steaming the vessel once again. Now only one of two operational side-wheelers in the UK, the little ex-River Dart steamer is based at Rochester and keenly supported by enthusiasts. She was built in 1924 by Philip & Son at Dartmouth, and was the final paddle steamer to be built for the River Dart Steam Boat Company. *Kingswear Castle* is still coal-fired, limited to 400 passengers in confined waters, and now the last river paddler to survive. Her engines were taken from a predecessor of the same name and were built in 1904. She was acquired in June 1967 by Paddle Steam Navigation, which is sponsored by the Paddle Steamer Preservation Society. The little steamer was returned to commercial work in 1985, thanks to the endeavours of many individuals and the generosity of industry; she now operates a seasonal commercial schedule on the

The *Kingswear Castle* (1924) at Tilbury on 26 June 1989. *Author*

Thames estuary, featuring most summer Saturdays and Sundays, and some additional weekday services as well.

In 1971 Meridian Line Cruises consolidated its position as provider of the below-bridge cruises by buying the *Swanage Queen* from Crosen of Poole to run alongside the *Eastern Princess*, formerly on Scroby Sands trips from Great Yarmouth. Of similar tonnage, about 106 gross, they were very different little ships, the *Swanage Queen* having been built in 1948 for service at Bridlington as the *Thornwick*, while the *Eastern Princess* was of wartime pedigree. They were mainly used for charters from Greenwich, but on summer Sundays the *Swanage Queen* operated a traditional public cruise from Tower Pier to Greenwich and Southend. Coakley's Launches' former Gosport steam ferry, the *Ferry Belle*, also occasionally called as far down-river as Southend during 1971. But the oddest call at Southend Pier was the British Rail train and passenger ferry *Vortigern*, which took a charter to Greenwich on 22 May 1971 – probably the largest vessel ever to berth at either pier.

One of the larger dedicated excursion ships to come to the Lower Thames in recent years is the *Princess Pocahontas*, which took up service in time for the 1990 season. Built in 1962 in Rendsburg, she is some 140 tons gross and can accommodate up to 300 passengers on a Class IV Certificate on short cruises from Gravesend, Tilbury and Southend. She is owned by the Freemen of the River Thames and is named after an Indian Princess reputedly buried at Gravesend.

The excursionists' preference in the 1980s and 1990s was day return trips via Dover or Folkestone to Calais or Boulogne. The only difference from the earlier days was that the family car came as well, allowing trips ashore. Before returning to the ferry at the end of the day, a visit to the Hypermarché allowed the car boot to be loaded with beer, wine and cheese, with more booze coming from the ship's duty-free shop on the voyage home. The 'booze cruise', as it became known, was severely hit when the European Commission withdrew the duty-free concession in 1999. The day excursion is still advertised with fares for a car together with up to five passengers typically at around £30 all in, but such was the importance of the duty-free shop that a number of ferries were withdrawn from the Dover to Calais route at the turn of the millennium.

One area that has thrived in recent years is the London tourist boats and bateaux mouches, which ply between the city piers. This all-year-round trade offers a range of boats, from small former Portsmouth Harbour ferries to large purpose-built multi-hull vessels. The reintroduction of commuter services, notably from Canary Wharf, has been less well received and services have tended to be short-lived.

The *Princess Pocahontas* (1962) below Tower Pier on the afternoon return leg down river on 24 September 2003. *Author*

'Above-bridge', the river services are offered from centres such as Oxford, Reading and Windsor using a variety of vessels, many of which are former steamers up to 100 years old, now equipped with noisy diesel units. However, their distinctive counter sterns and clipper stems reveal their heritage. One vessel, the *Streatley*, built in 1906, has recently been reunited with her original Sisson steam engine (Number 708) and steams along the river on corporate and family charters. Two others, the *Alaska* and the *Nuneham*, are also back in steam. The silence of their passage is quite remarkable and even the normally nervous swans remain undisturbed as the boats pass by.

This brings us to the summer of 2008. The former Isle of Wight motor ferry *Balmoral* graced the Thames piers in June and July. Her modern-day consort, the former London & North Eastern Railway Clyde paddle steamer *Waverley*, having missed her early-season duties on the Clyde with paddle trouble, operated in and around the Thames area during September and October. Long may these ships continue to offer these traditional excursion opportunities. The *Princess Pocahontas* offered short cruises from Gravesend down-river to Southend (although the pier was closed for much of the 2006 summer due to a fire), and up-river to the Pool of London (non-landing). The little paddle steamer *Kingswear Castle* offered trips on summer weekends and occasional weekdays, although mainly confined to the rivers Medway and Swale.

Once the motor coach took passengers from the pleasure steamers, then the car continued the erosion. Nowadays the Londoner's dream is no longer a day out to Clacton or Margate – the ideal is now provided by the low-cost airline and the prospect of a holiday in the sun. Never again will the cry of 'Gen'leman's lorst 'is 'at!' precede the sale of hat guards in very calm weather, and no longer will pennies be thrown by passengers down ventilator mouths! The 'Belles', the 'Eagles' and the 'Queens' are a thing of the past, but still remembered affectionately and talked about eagerly as passengers lean over the taff-rail of the *Waverley* as she glides alongside Clacton Pier.

One remarkable artefact still remains with us. Rescued from the breaker's yard and placed in a millpond on the Isle of Wight as a restaurant for some years, the ailing remains of Captain Shippick's *Medway Queen* now lie in poor condition on the Medway. Despite a prolonged and expensive programme of rehabilitation and restoration, funds were not able to keep abreast with the rot, and the future of this Dunkirk veteran was in doubt until the Lottery Fund recently granted more than £1 million towards her restoration. Her memory stays with us regardless: the smell from the engine room ports, the green foam around her paddle boxes, that lasting smell of stale beer and fried food that so characterised this class of ship, and the fresh tang of seaweed deep under the decking on Southend Pier – all this will stay with us for ever.

REFERENCES

Periodicals

Journal of Commerce, Motor Ship, Sea Breezes, Paddle Wheels, Cruising Monthly, The Illustrated London News

Books

Brodie, I. *Steamers of the Forth* (Newton Abbot: David & Charles, 1976)

Burtt, F. *Cross Channel and Coastal Passenger Steamers* (London: Richard Tilling, 1937)
Steamers of the Thames and Medway (London: Richard Tilling, 1949; reprinted by Roadmaster Publishing, Chatham, 1997)

Cope Cornford, L. *A Century of Sea Trading 1824-1924* (London: A. & C. Black Limited, 1924)

Coton, R. H. *A Decline of the Paddle Steamer* (York: The Paddle Steamer Preservation Society, 1971)

Dix, F. L. *Royal River Highway* (Newton Abbot: David & Charles, 1985)

Duckworth, C. L. D. and Langmuir, G. E. *West Highland Steamers* (3rd edition) (Prescot: T. Stephenson & Sons, 1967)
Clyde River and other Steamers (4th edition) (Glasgow: Brown, Son & Ferguson, 1990)

Farr, G. *West Country Passenger Steamers* (Prescot: T. Stephenson & Sons, 1967)

Grimshaw, G. *British Pleasure Steamers 1920-1939* (London: Richard Tilling, 1945)

Hambleton, F. C. *Famous Paddle Steamers* (London: Percival Marshall & Company, 1948)

Hancock, H. E. *Semper Fidelis: the Saga of the 'Navvies' (1924-1948)* (London: The General Steam Navigation Company, 1949)

Lyon, D. J. *The Denny List, Parts I and IV* (Greenwich: National Maritime Museum, 1975)

Machin, T. *MV Coronia Diamond Jubilee* (Scarborough: Carrick Publications, 1995)

McNeill, D. B. *Irish Passenger Steamship Services, Volume 2: South of Ireland* (Newton Abbot: David & Charles, 1971)

Palmer, S. '"The most indefatigable activity": the General Steam Navigation Company 1824-50', *The Journal of Transport History*, Vol 3, No 2, 1982, pp1-22

Paterson, A. J. S. *The Golden Years of the Clyde Steamers (1889-1914)* (Newton Abbot: David & Charles, 1969)

Plummer, R. *The Ships that Saved an Army* (Wellingborough: Patrick Stephens Limited, 1990)

Robins, N. S. *The British Excursion Ship* (Glasgow: Brown, Son & Ferguson, 1998)
Ferry Powerful: a History of the Modern British Diesel Ferry (Portishead: Bernard McCall, 2003)
Birds of the Sea: 150 Years of the General Steam Navigation Company (Portishead: Bernard McCall, 2007)

Robins, N. S. and Meek, D. E. *The Kingdom of MacBrayne* (Edinburgh: Birlinn Limited, 2006)

Sahlsten, R., Söderberg, B. and Bång, K. *Stena Line's Ships 1962-1992* (Gothenburg: Stena Line AB, 1992)

Sherwood, T. *The Steamboat Revolution: London's First Steamships* (Stroud: Tempus Publishing, 2007)

Smeaton, E. and Morris, G. *The General Steam Navigation Co Ltd* (Unpublished manuscript lodged with DP World P&O Heritage Collection, London, 1982)

Thornley, F. C. *Steamers of North Wales* (2nd edition) (Prescot: T. Stephenson & Sons, 1962)

Thornton, E. C. B. *Thames Coast Pleasure Steamers* (Prescot: T. Stephenson & Sons, 1972)

INDEX